THE MASTERS OF CAPITAL

THE YALE CHRONICLES
OF AMERICA SERIES

The
Masters
of Capital
A Chronicle
of
Wall Street
by
John Moody

1974
Toronto
Glasgow, Brook & Co.

New York
United States Publishers
Association, Inc.

CONTENTS

THE MASTERS OF CAPITAL

CHAPTER I

THE RISE OF THE HOUSE OF MORGAN

THE old meaning of the word "capital" — that is, an accumulation of wealth, either money or substantial property, for use in the production of more wealth — has been greatly enlarged within recent times. In earlier days, under the crude methods then prevailing, a given manufacturing plant might earn, say, ten per cent on its invested capital; but when power machinery and improved processes came into use and earnings increased, say, to twenty-five or forty per cent, the practice began of putting a valuation on this increased earning power, and the "value" of a given property, instead of being based on its original or replacement cost, came to be measured by its capacity to earn profits.

Upon this new basis, "capital," as expressed

through the issue of corporate stocks and bonds, was created by leaps and bounds. As the industry of the community became more efficient and the unit of effort brought forth greater results, corporate securities were created in an ever increasing ratio. Then, as the new custom became more firmly established, it was found that the limit of capitalization was by no means reached when *present* earning power alone was capitalized, for in a growing country like the United States, with population practically doubling every generation, future earning power was seen to be vastly greater. So the capitalists quite naturally took the further step and issued corporate stocks and bonds based on estimated future earnings.

Naturally, this modern practice of preëmpting or capitalizing probabilities was overdone. Such a process inevitably invited speculation; and "boom" periods, with recurring lapses and setbacks, became characteristic of the times. Eventually, the capitalists learned that this new capital, which represented not only accumulated wealth and current earnings but the future possible earning power of the community generally, must be bolstered up and insured by some artificial process. So long as normal growth in population and industry continued, the capitalists could feel fairly secure, but during industrial and banking crises, crop failures, or other adversities, the earnings of capital might decline to such a point as seriously to impair the valuation. Thus there arose among capitalists — large and small — a widespread demand for legislation and public aid to protect the integrity of the values which they had set up — a demand that customs tariffs be made more rigid than before to prevent foreign competition and for other measures to preserve the *status quo* of the new dispensation.

The railroads, during the decade after the Civil War, were the most conspicuous beneficiaries of the new process; but when inventions came in, such as the telephone and electric light and power, as well as numerous other devices for economizing time and labor, the current results and future possibilities of all these likewise were capitalized. In case of public utilities the supposed value of the franchise was made the primary basis of capitalization. In the quarter century from 1890 to 1915, the total capitalization in the form of stocks and bonds of public service corporations in the United States grew from less than two hundred million to nearly twenty billion dollars.

This new capitalism was a phenomenon of far-

reaching effect in financial circles. In the aggregate it represented in 1915 approximately one
hundred billion dollars in a nation whose entire
wealth was roughly estimated at something more
than twice this sum. When it is remembered that
just 25 years prior the wealth of the nation was
estimated at only sixty-five billions, and the corporate capital at that time was only about twenty-
five billions, the significance of the development
during the next generation will be appreciated.
And when it is further realized that in only one
half century not only a new system of capitalizing
wealth-producing forces has grown up, but also a
concentration of control in small groups of powerful
men, the subject becomes intensely interesting.

The great financial houses of Wall Street, which
have been most closely identified with the organization and control of the great corporate enterprises of the country, nearly all started as firms
engaged in the dry-goods or clothing business. Not
only the Morgans, but the Brown Brothers, Kuhn,
Loeb and Company, the Seligmans, and other
old private banking houses of New York, began
in this way. It was a natural beginning, for prior
to the period of modern machinery capital in large

masses was employed chiefly by merchants, and the wholesale handling of merchandise was among the most profitable of undertakings. Before the idea of capitalizing potential possibilities took possession of the minds of men, the purely competitive commercial business, such as the wholesale merchandising of goods, still held the center of the stage, both in this country and Europe. Even Nathan Rothschild, the most famous financier of the early nineteenth century, had made his start by financing the materials and products of the early English cotton mills. So also in America, the capital of the day tended to gather in the hands of great merchants whose stock in trade was very largely cloth or manufactures from cloth.

Most Americans have forgotten all this early history. Our "merchant princes" — in their heyday models of aspiration for every American boy — have passed out of mind. The business of security making and selling — in those days a small, local, irregular peddling trade as compared to the business of the big American merchant — now looms so large that it seems to have been always important. In England they remember better. The men whom we in this country call "private bankers," such as the Rothschilds, the Barings, and Morgans, have not always been known as bankers over there, but as "merchants." They are the lineal business descendants of the great East India Company of olden times.

In the United States one particular section developed the international merchant. Before the days of the American Revolution the sharp-eyed, bony men of New England had gone out scouring the coasts of Africa and the islands of the sea for merchandise. There were no better traders in the world than they, and there are probably no better traders than the Yankee now. Then, after the shipping troubles caused by the War of 1812, the men and money of New England turned to the new business of the manufacture of cloth; and thus was laid the foundation of the important cotton goods manufacturing industry in New England.

In the year 1811, a sixteen-year-old dry-goods clerk, George Peabody, was thrown out of employment by the burning of his brother's little store in the old town of Newburyport, Massachusetts. He then went with an uncle to Georgetown, D. C. (since incorporated with Washington), and opened a small retail dry-goods store there. After some years he moved to Baltimore and established branches in Philadelphia and New York.

Finally, in 1837, at the age of forty-two, he went to London and founded there the merchant banking house of George Peabody and Company, which later became J. S. Morgan and Company.

George Peabody's departure for London was not in itself notably interesting at the time. In London he continued to be a "merchant" just as he had been in this country, but in establishing himself in the greatest mercantile and banking center in the world he was really making an advance along unusual lines. The kind of enterprise he founded is excellently described by his biographer, Fox-Bourne:

In London and in parts of England, he bought British manufactures for shipment to the United States; and the ships came back freighted with every kind of American produce for sale in England. To that lucrative account, however, was added one far more lucrative. The merchants and manufacturers on both sides of the Atlantic, who transmitted their goods through him, sometimes procured from him advances on account of the goods in his possession long before they were sold. At other times they found it convenient to leave large sums in his hands long after the goods were disposed of, knowing that they could draw whenever they needed, and that in the meantime their money was being so profitably invested that they were certain of a proper interest on their loans. Thus he became a banker as well as a great merchant, and ultimately much more of a banker than a merchant.

In London, the chief financial center of the world, George Peabody represented the greatest and most profitable field for the investment of capital — the American continent, as yet practically unscratched. Literally millions of square miles of the richest farming and mineral lands were there to be had for the asking; valueless it is true until populated, but potentially of vast value. The men who acquired or preëmpted this vast El Dorado, equipped it with power machinery, and the means of transportation, thus setting labor to work, would create values which would mount for generations to come. Untold wealth would continuously flow into their coffers.

To English and continental capital this prospect was the dream of the ages. No such outlook or opportunity had ever come to England or the old countries. The natural resources of England were already preëmpted when modern inventions first began to come into use; the rich farming lands and rural regions, while undeveloped, were and for ages had been in the possession of a rich land-holding class; labor could not be applied to them and this later generation of capitalists found no extraordinary opportunities there for the production of wealth. Thus English capital inevitably turned to America, for America had few or no cash resources and any development of the country on a large scale must be carried out by those who had the means. There was little capital anywhere. Men were busily engaged, all along the Atlantic seaboard, making their living in the ordinary, old-fashioned way, and were not bent, to any great degree, on amassing large fortunes. The speculative era in America had not yet arrived, and, though manufacturing had begun, we were still — in the fourth decade of the century — a nation of planters and farmers.

When Peabody took up his residence in London, European capitalists were already competing for the opportunity to exploit American enterprises. Strong foreign houses were forming financial connections between London and New York. The Rothschilds had sent August Belmont to represent them in New York in the same year that Peabody had settled in London. The Barings had married into a Philadelphia family in the early years of the century and were also financially interested in the United States. Peabody, nevertheless, set out to be the chief representative of America in England. Every year he made a point of getting the leading men of both countries together, and his Fourth of July dinners in London grew to be notable occasions for promoting friendliness between the business interests of England and the United States.

Peabody never aspired to be an originator or promoter of enterprises. This work he left to others. His business was that of the financier, a "master of capital." In this field his success was enormous for the times, and his name grew constantly in English favor. He finally amassed a fortune of twenty million dollars, became the greatest philanthropist of his time, refused a title of nobility from Queen Victoria, and died in 1869 in the possession of the thorough confidence of the English investing public. After his death, his statue was set up in the London financial district, not far from the dingy little spot at Wanford Court which had been his office during his entire London business life.

When Peabody retired, in 1864, Junius S. Morgan became the head of the business. Morgan was another Yankee dry-goods trader — a member of the firm of J. M. Beebe and Company of Boston — who had been taken into partnership by Peabody ten years before. He was now about fifty-one and was fully capable of carrying on the high traditions of the Peabody firm — doing international commercial banking, holding deposits of customers, and buying and selling securities. The firm placed considerable issues of American railroad bonds in London and negotiated a loan to Chile. The name of George Peabody and Company ended with the death of Peabody, according to his own wish. But the business was carried on without interruption under the name of J. S. Morgan and Company.

Junius Morgan had a son, John Pierpont by name, born in Hartford, Connecticut, in 1837, when his father was in the dry-goods business there. This son was educated partly at the English High School in Boston and had finished his education at the University of Göttingen in Germany. After leaving the University he had entered his father's office in London. He was an extraordinary mathematician and had been strongly tempted to take up the career of professor of mathematics. But his father thought otherwise, and in the offices of George Peabody and Company young Pierpont got his first training in the technicalities of commercial banking and no doubt began the development of that unusual capacity for accurate and quick decision which so strongly characterized his entire career.

It was in 1857, the year of a great financial panic in the United States, that John Pierpont Morgan,

a tall, taciturn young man of twenty, stepped on
the stage of American business. At that time the
house of George Peabody and Company was doing
its American business through the New York firm
of Duncan, Sherman and Company, and this firm
was so seriously crippled in the financial crisis that
in order to save the situation George Peabody
and Company had to appeal to the Bank of England for assistance. This experience impressed the
London house with the vital importance of closer
control of its American business, and it was decided
to send young Pierpont Morgan to represent the
firm in New York as cashier of Duncan, Sherman
and Company.

In the offices of Duncan, Sherman and Company, Pierpont Morgan met Charles H. Dabney,
a partner in the firm and also the accountant. It
was through association with Dabney that Morgan acquired his remarkable and accurate knowledge of bookkeeping and accounting. But the connection of the Peabody firm with Duncan, Sherman
and Company was not destined to last very long.
In 1864, the year in which George Peabody retired
and was succeeded by Junius S. Morgan, Pierpont
Morgan and Dabney formed a new firm under the
name of Dabney, Morgan and Company, with

offices in Exchange Place, New York. This new firm became the correspondents of J. S. Morgan and Company of London. A few years later, Duncan, Sherman and Company failed and faded from view.

The house of Dabney, Morgan and Company built up an excellent business in foreign exchange and in the sale of miscellaneous securities and was no doubt financially successful, for when Dabney retired he was currently reported to have taken a substantial fortune out of the business. But the house had done nothing spectacular or striking; it was not classed with the big bankers of the Street; and its main prestige seems to have been based simply on its connection with the strong London firm of J. S. Morgan and Company. But in the year 1871 a change came. Dabney retired, the firm was dissolved, and young Morgan became a partner with the Drexels of Philadelphia, under the firm name of Drexel, Morgan and Company. Anthony J. Drexel, the senior partner, then personally bought the southeastern corner of Wall and Broad streets and built the Drexel Building, in which the new firm began its great career.

The Drexels were sons of a German portrait painter who had wandered about South America and Mexico carrying on his profession. In the course of his wanderings in the United States he had found that he could do a profitable business buying and selling state bank notes, which formed the "wildcat" currency of the time. In 1837, the same year in which Peabody moved to London, the elder Drexel had established himself in Philadelphia on a street known locally by the significant name of the "Coast of Algiers," where he laid the foundation of a great business in buying bank currency, "shaving" commercial paper, and financing corporations.

John Pierpont Morgan was thirty-four years old in 1871; Anthony Drexel, his principal partner, was forty-five — a conservative, intelligent, and popular man. There were four other members in the new firm, all from the Drexel house in Philadelphia. The new firm had advantageous alliances: on one side of the Atlantic, one of the richest financial houses in America; on the other, the great English house of J. S. Morgan and Company, in close touch with English capital — the greatest body of capital in the world. Its advantages were clear; but it also had its disadvantages. In the chief business of the day — the funding of the government debt — it came into a field already pretty well occupied.

Some years before the combination of the Drexels

and the Morgans had taken place and while Dabney, Morgan and Company were still doing a quiet banking business, a financial operation of vast magnitude had been carried on in America.   It was the flotation of the American Civil War debt.   This debt had been placed very largely through Jay Cooke, a Philadelphia banker and promoter.   Cooke was the typical American pioneer of his time, a tremendous optimist, a great employer of the benefits of friendship in high places, a sort of financial P. T. Barnum, who exploited the Government's securities and later his own.   He organized a great bond-selling campaign, giving "copy" to as many as eighteen hundred newspapers at a' time and canvassing through his agents every hamlet in the country.   Later, he was naturally the man who had the first opportunity to handle the great refunding operations in government bonds which were put through in 1871.

Thus, the house of Jay Cooke and Company had forged well to the front, and had built up very strong connections abroad.   During the Civil War period, English capital as a whole had not flowed very freely to the Northern States.   Tied to the South by the long established bonds of her cotton trade, the English were at first more inclined to buy Confederate than Union bonds. The Germans, however, as a whole were more sympathetic towards the North, as the great body of German immigrants following the uprising of 1848 were Northerners and strong supporters of the Union. And when the six per cent Union bonds had fallen to sixty cents on the dollar in gold, the Germans, and especially the wealthy South Germans, began to sell their own and invest in American securities. To German investors, America became the "land of ten per cent."

Jay Cooke estimated that by 1869 at least a billion dollars' worth of United States bonds were held abroad, of which a large proportion were held in South Germany. This large investment had established a new and powerful business interest in America — the German bond dealers, with foreign connections in the great European money center of Frankfort. With this new group of financial merchants Cooke had naturally allied himself, since the greatest source of English capital was only to be tapped through the Drexel-Morgan interests.

A keen contest arose between the Cooke interests (with their German connections) and the Drexel-Morgan interests to secure the contracts for the government financing. In this contest Cooke and his party won and then carried through an extraordinarily difficult operation so successfully that the Rothschilds offered themselves as Cooke's associates in future enterprises. But the Morgan interests kept after the business, and subsequently, in combination with Levi P. Morton, secured a half interest in the government refunding operation of 1873, involving a sale of $300,000,000 of bonds — an enormous transaction for those days. Later, in the fall of the same year, Jay Cooke and Company failed and this left the field in the United States for great financial operations entirely in the hands of the Drexel-Morgan-Morton associates.

By this time the house of Morgan had made great strides. But its position as the leading financial house of America had not come about alone through the downfall and eclipse of Jay Cooke and Company. A year before the formation of the Drexel-Morgan firm, an event of great importance had contributed vastly to the fame and standing of J. S. Morgan and Company. Toward the end of October, 1870, the city of London had been stirred by the news that J. S. Morgan and Company had taken a French loan of 250,000,000 francs. It was a syndicate operation and one of the largest and boldest ever known. In the previous month the Germans had crushed the French army at Sedan, had taken the Emperor Louis Napoleon prisoner, and had besieged Paris. The only authority for the loan was a provisional government at Tours. To take such a loan, even at the low price of about eighty, was undergoing some risk in view of the circumstances. One thing, however, was very clear: the hand of a strong, bold man was at the helm. The bonds were offered to the public at eighty-five; they advanced at once in price and within a year were selling fifteen points above what they cost the Morgan firm. And the syndicate was believed to have cleared $5,000,000 by the transaction. The reputation of the house of Morgan was thus well established among European bankers just at the moment when Pierpont Morgan, the son of Junius, came to the front in combination with the powerful Drexel interests, and just at the moment when foreign capital was ready to pour into America more freely than ever before. This was the opportunity of the house of Morgan. As the first big organizers of capital, the Morgans — father and son — were to wield a mighty influence in American finance.

CHAPTER II

MORGAN AND THE RAILROADS

THE work of Drexel, Morgan and Company in the refunding operations of the government debt, after the failure of Jay Cooke and Company, added greatly to American prestige abroad. For more than forty years the United States had been a burial ground for British capital. State bonds, Confederate bonds, railroad bonds, had proved to be disastrous investments. But now one single monumental success had restored faith in American securities. In all, about $750,000,000 of bonds were refunded, of which the Morgans handled a large part, and this achievement reopened America to British investors. In 1877 the financial magnates of America gathered in New York at a dinner to give thanks to Junius S. Morgan for "upholding unsullied the honor of America in the tabernacle of the old world," as Samuel J. Tilden, the toastmaster, expressed the sentiment of the hour.

By 1879, with the financing of the war debt accomplished, American bankers were ready to turn to a new field of activity.   But leadership in the dawning financial era was to fall to the younger men.   August Belmont, who represented the Rothschilds in America, was now sixty-three years old; Levi P. Morton, who had been Junius Morgan's fellow partner in the dry-goods firm of James M. Beebe and Company in Boston, was fifty-five; Junius Morgan himself, now sixty-six and presenting the ponderous figure of an East India merchant prince in an old English play, was retiring from active business life.   The younger Morgan was then forty-two, just about the age of George Peabody and Junius Morgan when they began their great careers in London.   Hitherto he had been merely the son of his grim-mouthed father. But he had learned the tools of his trade; he had watched and helped to operate great syndicates; and he was now well equipped to take his place in the security markets of America.

Pierpont Morgan had watched the expansion of the railroads for many years.   He had witnessed the most spectacular phenomenon of the period, for he had seen Gould and Vanderbilt accumulate their colossal fortunes largely by the manipulation of railroad properties. But he had taken little part in the battle of the railroads. Back in 1869, the firm of Dabney, Morgan and Company had helped to wrest from Gould and his accomplices the control of the Albany and Susquehanna Railroad, which was turned over to the Delaware and Hudson Canal Company. Again in 1878, when a rich comb manufacturer, Adolph Poppenhusen, had collapsed in the wild exploit of gridironing Long Island with railroad lines, Drexel, Morgan and Company picked up for a nominal sum his holdings, which were afterwards to be merged as parts of the Long Island Railroad. But aside from these minor incidents, the Morgan firm had not been active in railroad financing and were not in any sense known as railroad bankers.

In 1879, however, an incident occurred which brought Morgan directly into the field of railroad finance. William H. Vanderbilt, president and chief stockholder of the New York Central and Hudson River system, was then being harassed beyond endurance. Popular suspicion had been excited by his accumulation of a fortune of one hundred millions in ten years; and the New York Legislature, reflecting public indignation, was investigating the management of the New York

Central and was proposing radical control of railroad management. Besides, the rate wars between New York and Chicago were then raging. Finally, to add to these vexations, Jay Gould was attempting blackmail because Vanderbilt would not take him into the New York Central directorate. Vanderbilt's friends advised him strongly to dispose of a substantial portion of his stock in New York Central and thus avert the legislation that was aimed at him. But how to unload his vast holdings was a problem. To throw half of them on the market would result only in a panic; to distribute the stock by private sale in Wall Street would also greatly disturb values. Besides, what banker would undertake to put through such a gigantic transaction?

Vanderbilt consulted J. Pierpont Morgan, and Morgan devised a scheme whereby a large block of New York Central stock could be sold secretly in England without in any way disturbing the American security markets. This plan was adopted. The Morgan firm, through its London house, formed a syndicate and distributed 250,000 shares of the stock to permanent investors abroad. The transaction was kept secret for a time, but after a few months the details were all published in the New

York and the London papers. Vanderbilt then announced that a large part of the great sum of money he had received had been reinvested in United States government bonds. Thus, at one stroke, J. Pierpont Morgan not only solved Vanderbilt's difficult problem and allayed public criticism, but incidentally, it was said, he made a profit for his syndicate of more than three million dollars.

The financing of American railroads had been left hitherto largely in the hands of promoters whose primary interest had been to build the greatest possible amount of railroad, regardless of whether there was need for it or not, and sell it out for the highest possible price. This had been the programme in the halcyon days after the Civil War and in the speculative period following the panic of 1873. The Northern Pacific had been extended westward to the coast; the Atchison, Topeka and Santa Fé had been built through the deserts of Arizona and New Mexico; Gould had radiated his more or less dubious lines throughout sparsely settled sections west of the Mississippi; the Union Pacific had entered upon that policy of constructing or acquiring branch lines and feeders, which a few years later was its financial undoing. And in the East a no less reckless and ill-advised policy of construction had been going on. Most of the older systems were carried away with the idea of more and more mileage, more and more branches, more and more parallel lines. By the early eighties about twice as many railroad lines had been built as the country could profitably employ, and there had been issued about four times the amount of securities that the country could pay interest or dividends on. In 1884, Poor's *Manual*, the railroad authority of that time, stated with great positiveness that the entire capital stock of the railroads of the United States — then about four billion dollars — represented "water." It estimated that, in the three years ending December 31, 1883, two billions of capital and debt had been created, and that the "whole increase of share capital [about one billion] and a portion of the bonded debt was in excess of construction."

It was a crucial time for genuine investors, both at home and abroad. Thousands of these investors in Great Britain, on the Continent, and in the eastern parts of the United States, who had supplied, in one form or another, the cash for this vast promotion of the American transportation system, suddenly found their securities dwindling away. There was urgent need for a strong

representative to champion their interests.   After
his successful underwriting of the New York Central transaction, Morgan began to be looked upon as
a rescuer of investors, a solver of difficult financial
problems.   And he stood alone in this regard.   The
great railroad names of the period — Jay Gould,
Russell Sage, Collis P. Huntington, Calvin Brice,
and others — connoted expansion and speculation rather than wise control and conservative
management of railroad properties.

For a half dozen years the gigantic structure
of inflated railroad capitalization and over expansion stood — somewhat unsteadily — and then
the crash came.   By 1884 there were five independent lines operating between Chicago and the
Atlantic seaboard, and two more were building.
Three roads would have been ample for all the
business.   Railroad rates were torn to pieces; pas-
sengers traveled from New York to Chicago for
a dollar a head; grain was handled at an actual
loss of fifty per cent.   Three of these five roads were
tottering on the edge of bankruptcy, one had gone
bankrupt, and the New York Central was on the
verge of cutting down its dividends.   It was high
time for something of a constructive nature to
be done.

In the summer of 1885, William H. Vanderbilt
was again in dire need of a friend. The West Shore
Railroad was about to begin business as a competitor of the Vanderbilt lines. The Pennsylvania
Railroad interests were supposed to sympathize
with the West Shore project, for the reason that it
promised to embarrass seriously their chief competitor. At the same time Vanderbilt was support-
ing a project in Pennsylvania to parallel the main
line of the Pennsylvania Railroad. The West
Shore, according to the custom of the times, had
been heavily overcapitalized and, just as the road
was nearing completion, the company was dying
for want of cash. Unless the Pennsylvania interests
or some other strong capitalists should come to the
rescue, it evidently could not survive. Just at this
juncture Morgan came forward with the remedy.
He arranged to sell to the Pennsylvania interests
Vanderbilt's competing road in Pennsylvania and
to sell to the New York Central, practically at cost,
the West Shore Railroad.

Again, when the Philadelphia and Reading property, in which large amounts of English capital
had been sunk, was facing bankruptcy, a Morgan
syndicate furnished the millions needed for its
reorganization. In 1887, when the Baltimore and

Ohio Railroad was suddenly found to be also in a state of financial collapse, the Morgans stepped forward, found new capital for it, and commenced a policy of reconstruction — a policy, however, which was interrupted for a while by successful opposition from the old speculative interests. And a year later a Morgan syndicate reorganized the Chesapeake and Ohio.

Thus, before the panic of 1893, the firm of Drexel, Morgan and Company built up its reputation as the financier and reorganizer of mismanaged properties and in this respect stood in a unique position among American bankers. The great German security merchants had as yet little hold on American railways. The Rothschilds were content to remain a close ally of Morgan rather than a competitor, so far as the American field was concerned. Kuhn, Loeb and Company had not yet become a railroad power. The Speyers were strong but not masterful. The Seligmans, who had been prominent in the government refunding operations, had not become a leading house of issue for railway securities. Consequently, when more than half of the railroad mileage of the United States went into the hands of receivers, investors, both foreign and American, looked to one man and one house to defend their billions of investment in the railroads — the house of Morgan and its strong bold personality, John Pierpont Morgan, now known as "Jupiter" Morgan.

First came the reorganization of the Southern Railway. This system, whose connecting railroads had been snarled into an inextricable tangle under the Richmond and West Point Terminal control by a group of New York and Richmond speculators, fell into financial chaos. Morgan at first declined to have anything to do with the mess. But, others having tried in vain, the security holders finally besought Morgan to undertake the task on his own terms. In a comparatively short time a Morgan syndicate had reorganized the company, and long before the dire effects of the panic of 1893 and the ensuing depression had spent themselves, the Southern Railway system had advanced far on its new career of progress and prosperity.

It was not direct financial profit for himself or his firm that induced Morgan to undertake this reorganization; he was actuated by a larger, though not entirely unselfish, motive. He felt obliged in self-defense to see to it that the many millions of capital (especially that of English investors) should not be hopelessly wiped out. A firm whose greatest specialty was the marketing of American securities abroad could not afford to have these securities pass as worthless paper before the eyes of the world. The fame of the house of Morgan in London and all its traditions were based on the greatness and wealth of America, and both the Morgans, father and son, had always been "bulls on America."

With the successful reorganization of the Southern system, Morgan at last had a firm grip upon that slippery thing, the American railroad corporation. For forty years American railroad promoters, reckless optimists, gigantic thieves, huge confidence men — magnified a hundred times by the size of their transactions — had juggled and manipulated and exploited this great business for their own profit and the general loss of every one else concerned. Morgan had been watching for twenty years this manipulation of railroad property. The control of the properties lay in the voting power of the stock; and, if the voting power could not be controlled, little could be accomplished against opposition. His attempt to reconstruct the Baltimore and Ohio in 1887 was defeated entirely because the controlling interests checkmated him by voting his representative out. He devised a plan whereby he himself would control the voting power. Before undertaking a reorganization or finding the new capital, he provided for a "voting trust," a device which, for a number of years, placed in the hands of a few trustees selected by himself the entire voting power of the stock. This scheme was followed in the reorganization of the Southern Railway and was adopted in all later instances.

The next drastic reorganization was that of the Erie system. Before undertaking this task Morgan was particularly careful to concentrate control in his own hands. Years before, J. S. Morgan and Company had been the fiscal agents of the Erie in London and had placed large amounts of Erie bonds among British investors. Morgan was therefore particularly anxious to protect these bond-holders, and in the scheme which he devised he saw that these bondholders themselves got enough voting power to outvote the scattered stockholders, though even the bondholders were controlled for the time being by a Morgan "voting trust." It was only fair that the stockholders rather than the bondholders should suffer in the Erie reorganization, because the great issues of Erie stock created during the gambling days of Drew, Fisk, and Gould represented little or no cash investment, while the bonds had, for the most part, been issued for the payment of actual property.

Other Morgan reorganizations now followed apace. The Hocking Valley, a system of roads in the Middle West, was placed on its feet; the Northern Pacific, after its checkered career of thirty years of construction, collapse, and manipulation, finally found permanent lodgment in the capacious arms of the firm of Morgan. The Baltimore and Ohio, the Atchison, Topeka and Santa Fé, and several other large properties, although not exclusively reorganized by the Morgans, came to life again partially as a result of their work. The Philadelphia and Reading system, an acute sufferer from the wild gambling spirit of the previous decade, was also taken in hand for the second time, and with a strong financial organization started on its career as the dominating factor in the anthracite coal combination; and other properties not completely wrecked in the smash of 1893, among them the Lehigh Valley and the Central of Georgia, were likewise rejuvenated.

Pierpont Morgan was by 1898 a towering figure in the railroad and banking world. He had largely reorganized the railroad system of America. He was in complete voting control of the great network of lines radiating throughout the South Atlantic seaboard; he entirely dominated the Erie Railroad; he was the chief factor in the policy of the Reading; he controlled the vast Northern Pacific; he had a powerful voice in the administration of the Baltimore and Ohio and also an important interest in the affairs of the Atchison, Topeka and Santa Fé; he had the entire capital stock of the rejuvenated Central of Georgia locked up in his safe; he controlled the Hocking Valley, the Chesapeake and Ohio; and he was the real financial power behind the vast system of the Vanderbilt lines.

Credit must of course be given to other men for a substantial share in this great work. Aside from the Drexels, Morgan had been fortunate for years in securing the aid of partners of no mean ability. Perhaps he trained them; perhaps their qualities developed as a result of the environment in which he placed them. In any event, in these earlier years, several names stand out prominently. One of these is Egisto P. Fabbri, a native of Italy, who became Morgan's partner in 1876 and continued until 1884. Other conspicuous names in these and later days were J. Hood Wright, Charles H. Godfrey, George S. Bowdoin, and Charles H. Coster. All these men either retired rich in middle life or died in harness. Coster was a notable example of a man who worked himself to death. He was a great master of detail, besides being a genius at working out plans of reorganization. It is asserted that all the successful Morgan reorganization plans up to the time 'of Coster's death were his work. Perhaps this is true; at any rate during these trying years Coster was Morgan's right arm. He was a familiar figure in Wall Street — a white-faced, nervous man, hurrying from meeting to meeting and at evening carrying home his portfolios. He traveled across the country, studying railroad systems, watching roadbeds from the back platforms of trains, evidently never getting a chance for rest or leisure. When he died suddenly in the spring of 1900, the newspapers pointed out that he had been a director in fifty-nine corporations.

And now, as the period of railroad reorganization closed and a new century was at hand, the house of Morgan once more found itself with only one commanding figure in its list of American partners. Fabbri was dead; J. Hood Wright was dead; Charles H. Coster was dead; Walter Burns, the London genius who had handled affairs there since the demise of the elder Morgan, was also dead — all having succumbed to the gigantic, nerve-racking business and pressure of the Morgan methods and the strain involved in the care of the railroad capital of America. Both the Drexels were also gone. "Jupiter" Morgan had alone come through that soul-crushing mill of business, retaining his health, vigor, and energy.

CHAPTER III

THE IRONMASTERS

ANDREW CARNEGIE came to America with his father, mother, and brother in 1848, when he was thirteen years old. His parents were utterly penniless. They gravitated to Allegheny, where the father secured work in a cotton mill, and young Andy became a bobbin boy at one dollar and twenty cents a week. His mother helped out by taking in washing and binding boots for a shoemaker named Phipps, who had a small shop near by. This shoemaker had a ten-year-old son called Harry, and there it was that the two small boys, Henry Phipps and Andrew Carnegie, laid the foundations of their long friendship.

Andy worked as bobbin boy for a year, then became a stoker, and finally, at fifteen, he secured a job as a telegraph messenger boy at three dollars a week. He soon learned how to send and receive messages, often practising with other boys before the operator arrived in the morning. He had not been a messenger boy long before he displayed the striking quality which so characterized him in after life — audacity. The boys were forbidden to touch the instruments, but it one day happened that an important message came over the wires when the operator was out. Andy jumped to the instrument and took the message. For this breaking of orders he was not only forgiven but was promoted to be an operator at a salary of six dollars a week. A few years later, his industrious efforts and efficient work came under the notice of Colonel Thomas A. Scott, who was general superintendent of the Pennsylvania Railroad in Pittsburgh, and young Carnegie soon became a railroad telegraph operator at a further increase in salary. He was now nineteen years old, and his audacity and initiative began to develop rapidly. One day, during the absence of Colonel Scott, an accident occurred on the lines, which tied up the traffic. Immediately Carnegie wrote a dozen telegrams, containing orders for setting the trains in motion and signed them all "Thomas A. Scott." This saved the day, and Scott, who recognized the great qualities in the lad, made him his private secretary.

From the beginning of Colonel Scott's friendship,

Carnegie's future was assured. In his new environment, he gained a wider outlook on life, and especially on business life, for Scott was an influential man in Pittsburgh and had his fingers in all sorts of business and speculative pies. Carnegie's first money was made in an oil speculation, without the investment of a cent of his own. He gave his note for a block of stock in one of the smaller Pennsylvania oil companies and then paid the note out of dividends received on the stock within a single year. This gave him a little capital and, under the guidance of Scott, he began to buy, with his small funds and with borrowed capital, shares here and there in many enterprises. Most of these enterprises were things in which Scott was an "insider" and thus Carnegie was able to make safe speculations on "sure enough" information. In a little while, he was the owner of shares in such companies as the Columbia Oil Company, the Woodruff Sleeping Car Company, the Pittsburgh Elevator Company, the Citizens' Passenger Railroad Company, and the Third National Bank of Pittsburgh.

For ten years Carnegie continued at his work as Scott's secretary and steadily added to his investments and his capital. In 1864, when he was twenty-eight, he succeeded Colonel Scott as superintendent of the railroad. But young Carnegie never planned to remain a mere employee of a railroad or any other corporation. He meant, as soon as his funds were sufficiently large, to have a business of his own. His eyes and ears were always open, and he watched his chances, profiting by the inside information he obtained as Scott's secretary. At first he had thought seriously of entering the oil business on his own account; but evidently no real opportunity presented itself and he resolved to bide his time.

While the Civil War was drawing to a close, the country about Pittsburgh was being agitated not only by the petroleum boom, but by another type of industry, which, like the oil business, was also to leave its stamp on the economic life of America. This was the manufacture of malleable steel by the newly developed Bessemer process. Up to this time not a yard of railroad track in the United States had been laid with steel. American railroads were then iron roads. There were frequent references in those days to the "iron horse," and "iron roads." But iron was really too poor a metal for railroad rails, and men were constantly looking for something harder and more durable. Steel had been made for many years in small quantities, but the cost was far too great to bring it into general use. Moreover, the demand, even for iron, had not developed far enough to attract capital in any great amount. Iron was produced in small furnaces and in small quantities, and no one dreamed that it would ever become anything more than the precarious, poverty-stricken, uncertain industry that it had always been. The best furnaces in those days did not produce a thousand tons of iron a year; and, because of the fluctuations in demand, most iron makers were without capital and constantly in debt. The panics of 1837 and 1857 had caused the failure of scores of iron founders. Nobody with capital wanted to put money into so precarious a business.

But, as railroad building expanded, the demand for more durable iron began to increase steadily. Steel was recognized as the ideal substance for rails, but the cost of making it was prohibitive. If some genius would only devise a method for making cheap steel, he would be one of the benefactors of the century. And it usually happens, when the demand for a given thing is insistent enough, that the needed genius does arise. In 1847, a young man of thirty-six, William Kelly, bought the Suwanee Iron Works near Eddyville, Kentucky.

Kelly was an inventive character, but a poor business man. He desired to specialize on good, high class wrought iron for sugar kettles. To do this he invented a new method for making larger kettles, which soon became famous as "Kelly's Kettles." But the process was the old slow one of using charcoal in large quantities — a process which involved much time and enormous quantities of charcoal.

Almost by accident Kelly discovered that there was no need of charcoal; that air, too, was fuel. Every iron worker from time immemorial had believed that cold air would chill hot iron. But Kelly was something of a student of metallurgy and he knew that carbon and oxygen had an affinity for each other. Therefore when one day he saw his yellow mass of molten metal turn to a white heat without charcoal, and simply because of the air which happened to strike it, the truth flashed across his mind in an instant. Of course, it was as simple as breathing. When the air was blown into the molten metal, the oxygen united with the impurities of the iron and left the pure iron behind. Kelly was carried away with his discovery and immediately proclaimed it to an incredulous public. Instead of being rewarded, he was ridiculed. He found it impossible to convince any one that he was sane, and his business was finally ruined because buyers of iron refused to take his goods unless they "were made in the regular way." But Kelly persisted in his work, and within a few years he was actually producing malleable iron in substantial quantities.

But it took more than Kelly's discovery to bring steel into use on any large scale. The process he had worked out had to be put into general use and accepted abroad before American users of steel would have much to do with American-made steel. Hitherto practically all the steel used in America had been imported from England, and the tradition held that steel was essentially an English product and not a domestic article. Hence most people looked upon American-made steel as bogus and regarded the imported as the only real article. While Kelly was experimenting, an Englishman, by the name of Henry Bessemer, was also following out the same idea. And soon, "Bessemer" steel began to appear in small quantities in the United States. It was the same thing that Kelly had been making since 1847 by the same process; but whereas buyers at once accepted the imported "Bessemer steel," they still remained prejudiced against Kelly's "fool-steel."

After this, Kelly's career was a checkered one. It was not until many years afterwards that he was really recognized as the discoverer of the process in the United States. He finally secured a patent but lost it through bad business management, and it was long after the close of the Civil War before he got any financial benefits for his work. Ultimately, however, he was given full credit by the world at large for his services to the industry, and he is now universally recognized as having discovered and perfected the Bessemer process well in advance of Sir Henry Bessemer; although the Englishman brought his work to fruition far more rapidly.

During the latter days of the Civil War, with big plans pending for the construction of the Pacific railroads, the demand for railroad iron was taxing all the plants in the country. And, as the cost of production was falling to a point where it was commercially possible for steel to be used, capital in substantial quantities was seeking investment in this new industry. It seemed at last as if the iron industry might develop into a big money-making enterprise after all. And so thought Andrew Carnegie, for in May, 1864, we find him buying from Thomas N. Miller for $8920 a one-sixth interest in the Iron City Forge Company. The other stockholders at that time were Carnegie's boyhood friend, Henry Phipps, and Andrew Kloman. At about the same time Carnegie formed the Keystone Bridge Company, inducing J. Edgar Thomson, Colonel Scott, and other railroad officials to join him in financing the enterprise. It proved immediately successful, and in four years Carnegie had paid for his own stock out of the profits. The backing of the Pennsylvania Railroad, which Carnegie had shrewdly procured, was a gold mine to him. This road was building steel bridges by the score at this time, and of course the Keystone Bridge Company got all the business it could handle.

After the Civil War, when prices fell, Carnegie's steel business suffered reverses, but the bad times were tided over. When business revived, Carnegie emerged in complete control of the enterprise, having bought out Kloman and Miller, and the company never experienced real trouble again. Andrew Carnegie made money with great rapidity and long before the panic of 1873 he was a millionaire several times over and one of the big ironmasters of America.

It has often been asserted that Andrew Carnegie was the first American ironmaster to make steel by the Bessemer process. But this is not true. Carnegie was not a pioneer in this industry any more than John D. Rockefeller was in the oil business. Like Rockefeller, he took no real interest in a new idea until its practicality and future success had been well demonstrated by others. When Carnegie went into the iron business in 1864, he was still wedded to the idea that wrought iron, made by the old process, was to be the standard railroad metal of the future. But by 1866, many manufacturers were turning to the Bessemer process with evident success. At this time, William Coleman, one of his partners, suggested that they begin making steel by the Bessemer process. The other partners agreed, but Carnegie strenuously objected. Indeed, Carnegie was not a steel or iron expert in the real sense. He was a financier, a capitalist, a business booster. As his business developed, he spent less and less time in the management of the concern, and gave his best attention to popularizing the Carnegie products among buyers throughout the country. He promptly removed to New York and began to make the acquaintance of all kinds of people with a view to gathering prestige for himself and his business. He traveled widely and began to make many trips to Europe. In England he soon heard of Bessemer steel and realized that perhaps after all the new process was a sound one that should be adopted. Investigation thoroughly converted him to the idea. He rushed back to Pittsburgh and to the astonishment of his partners talked nothing but steel, steel, steel. Immediately the firm of Carnegie, McCandless and Company was formed with a capital of seven hundred thousand dollars. Carnegie subscribed the bulk of the amount needed and steps were at once taken for the construction of a large plant.

The new plant was situated a few miles from Pittsburgh and was named the Edgar Thomson Works, after the president of the Pennsylvania Railroad. This was another shrewd, calculating move on the part of Carnegie, who wished to get all the orders and advantages that could be obtained from this big consumer of steel rails. Moreover these were days of little or no railroad regulation, and railroad rebating was customary in both the oil and steel business. In fact, any large shippers could usually obtain rebates from the railroads to the disadvantage of the little shippers. In this way, also, Carnegie felt that a close relationship with the officials of the Pennsylvania Railroad would be an asset of value.

About the time that Carnegie was getting his money ready to buy out the Iron City Forge Company, in 1864 a fourteen-year-old lad named Henry Clay Frick was working as errand boy in a village store at Mount Pleasant, about forty miles from Pittsburgh. He was the son of poor parents, whose ancestors had emigrated from Switzerland more than a century before, a quiet, thoughtful lad, self-contained and reticent. In those days a new industry was developing at Mount Pleasant, known as coke making. Coal was mined and baked in brick ovens until it turned into crisp gray lumps. These lumps were very valuable to iron makers, who used them in smelting the iron ore. It is not probable that young Frick fully realized what developments were ahead in the iron and steel business of the country or that he foresaw the age of steel in which coke making would become a giant industry. But the boy saw in coke making a lucrative opportunity and began to save his money with the hope that in time he would have capital enough to buy a small strip of coal land and go into the business himself. In four or five years he had saved enough to buy a little coal land, and he then induced his grandfather and uncle to buy some ovens which were offered for sale at a low price. But shortly afterwards the panic of 1873 set in, and the little enterprise was balked. Frick had to continue working on a small salary and became bookkeeper for his grandfather, who was in the distillery business.

Young Frick had that audacity which is characteristic of successful men, and particularly of men who have made and developed great enterprises in America. Carnegie displayed this trait at the outset of his career, when he disobeyed orders to save a railroad wreck; Rockefeller displayed it when he plunged into the oil business with his little savings of seven hundred dollars; Pierpont Morgan displayed it in early life and it was his chief characteristic all through his long, active career. One day, after the smoke of the 1873 panic had disappeared and business was reviving, a Pittsburgh banker named Mellon received by mail a request for a loan of twenty thousand dollars from an unknown person by the name of H. C. Frick. No security was offered but big profits were promised if the money was advanced at once. The banker liked the tone of the letter and sent his partner to Mount Pleasant to investigate. Naturally he expected to meet a man of wealth and property and was surprised to find that "H. C. Frick" was merely a youth who was working for a few dollars a week and living in one room of a coal miner's house. But the banker had himself worked up from poverty; he liked the honest, bright face of the youth and was impressed with his sincerity and intelligence. Careful investigation confirmed his first impression, and the final result was that the twenty thousand dollars was advanced to the young operator.

Within a short time Frick became the foremost coke maker in the neighborhood. The price of coke kept rising in response to the great demand from the steel makers, and in one year Frick and his associates made a profit of one hundred per cent on their capital. All the profits went back into the business for the purchase of more coal lands and the building of more ovens. In a little while Frick was the coke king of Connellsville and was piling his profits up into the millions. He was more than a mere coke maker, however; he was an organizer of the highest type. He brought order out of chaos in the coke business; he induced his leading competitors to combine with him, thus eliminating cutthroat competition; he also settled troublesome labor problems by importing Hungarians and Slavs. His labor wars were not so much questions of wages as of law and order. On the whole he raised wages and improved the villages and mines in his region; but he was determined to be the master of his own business.

When in 1882 the tendency toward consolidation of interests had begun, it was natural enough that the coke making and the steel manufacturing businesses should be drawn together. Both Frick and Carnegie recognized the logic of the idea. Consequently in this year Carnegie and his associates bought control of the H. C. Frick Coal and Coke Company. This change of ownership brought Henry C. Frick into the steel business. He acquired a substantial interest in the Carnegie Works and an influence which became more evident from year to year. His intelligence and masterful qualities were exactly what the Carnegie organization needed. A new chapter now opened in the affairs of the company. Having acquired control of one raw material by purchasing the coke business, the company was now to make a further advance and acquire ore beds. And, as the only ore deposits of value were far from Pittsburgh in the Lake Superior region, it became necessary for the company to go into the transportation business also, to establish steamship lines on the Great Lakes and to build railroads from the water to its works at Pittsburgh.

The Mesaba ore fields, acquired by the Carnegie associates, had been first opened up by Louis Merritt, who had sold his holdings to John D. Rockefeller some years before. Rockefeller, knowing little at that time outside of the petroleum field, afterwards thought he had made a bad investment. But this was not the impression in Pittsburgh, where the possibilities of wealth in the mining of Lake Superior ore had now been fully recognized. A man named Harry Oliver, who had been in the steel business and had been a friend of Carnegie in his early days, realized the possibilities of the Mesaba Range and bought a large tract of land there for a small sum of money. Soon afterward Frick met Oliver on the street and suggested that the Carnegie company go into the Mesaba ore business with him. The terms suggested by Frick were that Oliver should surrender five-sixths of his stock, in return for which the Carnegie company would advance half a million dollars for the development of the mines. The bargain was made, and thus the Carnegie company acquired a property which in a few years was worth tens of millions of dollars. But this was only one step in the control of the ore supply. A few years later, Frick and Oliver joined forces with John D. Rockefeller in the Lake Superior ore business. This powerful alliance caused a great fall in the price of iron ore and forced many smaller producers to the wall. Their holdings were thereupon bought in by the Frick and Rockefeller combination.

Thus from small beginnings the steel business had grown into a gigantic industry. Meanwhile railroads had spread over the continent and the petroleum business had become a monopoly under the control of the Rockefellers. The time was at hand when the big bankers of Wall Street, already busy in the railroad field, would take part also in petroleum, steel, and a multitude of other industrial enterprises and utilities which had so grown in size and value that they could no longer remain independent of vast banking interests.

CHAPTER IV

STANDARD OIL AND WALL STREET

In 1859, ten years after the discovery of gold in California, another epoch-making discovery was made, this time in Pennsylvania. An enterprising prospector in Venango County drilled a well and produced a flow of petroleum, which was already known to have great commercial value. It was almost like finding liquid gold, for the stuff brought twenty dollars a barrel and it flowed at the rate of twenty-five barrels a day. In a few months' time the narrow valley in northwestern Pennsylvania where the discovery was made swarmed with madmen tearing open the ground in the frenzy of competition that characterizes all new mining districts. So far as was known, the petroleum might soon dry up and every one was hurrying to "strike oil" before it should be gone.

About this time a young commission merchant in Cleveland, Ohio, named John D. Rockefeller, had saved up about seven hundred dollars, nursing it from nothing, a few dollars at a time. In 1860 he took a chance with three other men in the venture of mining petroleum, putting in a portion of his seven hundred dollars. Within two years the three men had run their investment up to about four thousand dollars. They made a good burning oil, and their profits, like those of all refiners at the time, were amazingly large. During the next few years, tens of thousands of dollars were made annually by this concern. But instead of drawing these profits out, Rockefeller, who dominated the combination from the start, insisted that every cent possible be reinvested in the business. "Take out what you've got to have to live on, but leave the rest in," he kept urging his partners. "Don't buy new clothes and fast horses; let your wife wear her last year's bonnet. You can't find any place where money will earn what it does here."

And this was true. But this new business had peculiar risks. In the first place, the operators had no experience to guide them. Indeed, no one knew when this petroleum would give out; many feared that it would be exhausted in a few years and that they would be left with useless plants on their hands. In the second place, it faced the reckless competition of all enterprises promising fabulous profits. Rockefeller was farseeing enough to realize these dangers and shrewd enough to prepare for them. Thus he early advocated the theory that the oil business could only be made secure if bolstered up at all times by large cash reserves. He saw that, should more petroleum be discovered and the business continue on a large scale, only those concerns which had the immediate cash resources could hope ultimately to dominate the field. The producers and refiners who dissipated or spent their profits as they made them would have to succumb in the end to the stronger financial interests in the same field of activity.

Hence, during the period when the business was getting well established, the decade from 1860 to 1870, John D. Rockefeller and his friends year by year added steadily and quietly to their cash, until by 1867 they were in no sense dependent on bankers or financiers, as were the railroads and other large industries of the country. They were their own bankers from the start and were in a position even in those early days to snap their fingers at Wall Street and Lombard Street. When the Standard Oil Company of Ohio was formed in 1870 with one million dollars cash capital, it was undoubtedly the one great business corporation of America which had no debts and no direct banking alliances or affiliations.

There was, of course, a reason for this complete absence of banking or investing interest, aside from the announced policy of the Rockefeller group. From the beginning, such banking houses as the Morgans, the Drexels, and the foreign houses with American connections, had kept away from this new business, just as, until the twentieth century, conservative capital in Wall Street to a large extent kept away from precarious industries like copper mining, electrical enterprises, and so forth. The industry had not proved its permanence or stability and was therefore classed as a "speculation" rather than a sure investment.

Rockefeller was farseeing enough to divine this attitude and to take advantage of it by so forming his policy that, if the industry should demonstrate its permanent strength and earning power, he and his associates would reap all advantages and would never have to divide profits with banking interests or capitalists, in order to procure funds to carry the business through lean or unprofitable periods, as the railroad corporations had been forced to do. Not long after 1870 the wisdom of this policy was demonstrated. Hard times came, and refiners in all parts of the country went to the wall for want of cash. Bankers would not help them because of the newness and precarious nature of the business. Then the Standard Oil Company began to buy the weaker refineries at bargain prices and to establish a chain of plants across the country. This enabled it to organize production on a large scale and to reduce the cost of refining and distributing oil to a fraction of what it cost most of its competitors. The company then bought the pipes which connected the wells in all parts of the country and laid miles and miles of pipe lines of its own. This forced the railroads to come to terms, as they had been large shippers of oil; and they were obliged to accede to a policy of secret rebating in the interest of Standard Oil and at the expense of the independent refiners. Ultimately, nearly all the competition in the oil trade was eliminated by these methods, until, in 1879, the Standard Oil interests were the only bona-fide buyers, the only gatherers, and the only refiners of all but ten per cent of the petroleum of the country. One by one, all the plants in the business without sufficient cash capital had fallen into the hands of the one firm supplied with cash.

During the decade in which this expansion of the Standard Oil Company took place, the policy was never abandoned of accumulating and retaining large cash resources. By 1875 the cash resources had risen from about one million in 1870 to over thirteen millions; half a dozen years later they reached forty-five millions; and during that decade the company and its subsidiaries had not only bought up most of their competitors with ready cash but in addition had paid out in dividends over eleven million dollars.

Up to this period, most men had not foreseen the possibilities of the petroleum industry. Least of all had they thought of its bringing about a concentration of capital. The great bankers who were coming to the front, such as Jay Cooke and Company, Drexel, Morgan and Company, and the varied representatives of German and Dutch capital in the United States were concentrating their attention almost exclusively on the development of steam railroads. The achievements of the Cookes and of the Morgans and their colleagues were the financing of governments and of railroads. This fact remained true long after the Standard Oil Trust had taken its place as the most powerful "master of capital" on the continent. Thus while the banking interests of America, as represented by the Morgan type, were rising, there was also growing a new banking power which for a long time they persistently ignored. Adherence to the Rockefeller policy meant that the Standard Oil capitalists must organize in such a manner as to perform banking functions; so the Standard Oil Company of Ohio was from its very inception its own banker. As this industry spread and subsidiaries were formed in various States, it became necessary to have the vast financial operations handled from one central head. The New York office was then organized and became the financial center of the business. The numerous subsidiary companies all became responsible to the New York office, and all the cash and surplus funds gravitated to that point.

With the year 1882 begins the period when the Standard Oil capitalists began to make their influence more directly felt in Wall Street. In that year was formed the famous Standard Oil Trust and "26 Broadway" became the official financial and business center of the petroleum industry of the country. In a little while, the Standard Oil Trust was really a bank of the most gigantic character — a bank within an industry, financing this industry against all competition and continually lending vast sums of money to needy borrowers on high class collateral, just as the other great banks were doing.

Standard Oil was swelling with cash assets, and the small group of men who controlled its destinies had become multimillionaires. Of the dividends of over eleven million dollars distributed between 1870 and 1882, John D. Rockefeller had received the bulk, but Oliver H. Payne, Henry M. Flagler, William Rockefeller, and a few others received a substantial remainder. Naturally these new millionaires sought investment for their fabulous incomes, aside from such portions of them as they were able to reinvest in the oil industry. They were soon impelled to turn to other fields of enterprise, not only to employ their own funds profitably but to find investment for the steadily swelling surpluses and cash assets of the Standard Oil Company itself.

Far back in the period prior to the Civil War the great West India trading house of G. G. and S. Howland was doing business at the foot of Wall Street. The last and possibly the greatest of the old school of New York merchants — Moses Taylor — served his apprenticeship there. He had been brought up in the strictest traditions of the old-style merchants, for his father had been confidential agent for the old fur trader, John Jacob Astor. In 1832, when Taylor was twenty-six years old, he started in the West India business for himself and became the chief figure in the great raw sugar trade. In 1855 he became president of the old City Bank — the bank of the merchants of raw materials.

The rich Cuban planters deposited their money with him and left in his care the reams of United States government bonds into which they had put their savings. The bank had also a strong cotton clientèle, and it handled the business of such houses as the great importing metal firm of Phelps, Dodge and Company. It was even then what a strong bank should be — a federation of interests still stronger and greater than itself.[1]

---

[1] In those days, the different classes of merchants had their particular banks, as indeed they have today to some extent. To the north of Wall Street, towards the East River, where the tanyards lay in the "swamp," were the banks of the leather merchants. The banks of the dry-goods trade — such as the Park and the Chemical — kept near these merchants as they edged up Broadway. The leading bank of the raw materials' merchants — the City Bank — stayed where it was first founded in 1812, in the old center, the ancient banking row on the north side of Wall Street. It did not grow so fast as the banks of the dry-goods merchants, but it was destined in the end to outstrip all.

Moses Taylor had his own ideas about running a bank. First of all, it must be strong; his cash reserve was his pride. The City Bank always had a great holding of surplus cash. Whenever there is a panic, everybody puts his money in the safest place he knows. Moses Taylor's bank was safe and strong; with every panic it grew stronger. The story of the City Bank from the time Taylor took charge of it is a record of steady appreciation in credit and reputation. Behind it stood Moses Taylor, with his enormous private fortune which was estimated at fifty millions when he died in 1882. During that period Wall Street had grown out of its swaddling clothes and had become a center of finance and commerce far outreaching that of any other city in the country. In the neighborhood of the City Bank, and doing active business with it, were still the sugar merchants, the cotton brokers, the metal merchants, to whom had been added, as the years went on, the important anthracite coal interests, the leading New York gas companies, and some of the railway companies of the South and West.

When Moses Taylor died, the future of the City Bank, as the strongest if not the largest institution of its kind, was for a time uncertain. Percy R.

Pyne, a kindly, gentle man, who had charge of the Taylor mercantile interests, ran the bank for the next nine years; but during his administration no startling developments took place. The bank held its own; that was all. But, with the death of Pyne in 1891, a real "master of capital" appeared as the head of this famous bank. James Stillman was born in Brownsville, Texas, in 1850, of New England parents. He was a shy, reticent child, trained from the first in the virtues and customs of the old school merchant class. One of his earliest playthings, which he always preserved, was a toy bank, across the front of which he had printed "City Bank," his father having been associated with Moses Taylor and the City Bank interests. During his teens his father was stricken with paralysis, and young Stillman was thrown on his own resources. At the age of twenty-one he was a member of the firm of Smith, Woodward and Stillman, cotton commission merchants on South Street, near Wall. But Stillman did not care for ordinary mercantile business. While his partners were actively carrying on the mercantile end of the business with great success, he associated himself more and more with men of financial knowledge and power. In the early eighties, he was elected to the board of directors of the Chicago, Milwaukee and St. Paul Railroad, which was then seeking stronger financial connections. At the same time William Rockefeller — whose bulging cash assets, as well as his brother John's, were looking for an outlet — James T. Woodward, president of the Hanover National Bank, and Philip D. Armour, the great packer of the Middle West, were elected to the same board.

Association on the board of directors of the St. Paul property brought Stillman and Rockefeller together, and their intimacy grew closer when in 1885 William Rockefeller was induced to become a director of the Hanover Bank of which Stillman was also a director. They became personal friends as well as business associates; and when in 1891 the presidency of the City Bank was offered Stillman, the Rockefeller business naturally began to gravitate to that institution. But no one realized at that time that Stillman was a great banking genius or was consciously planning the union of two great interests with the same policy of accumulating heavy cash resources — the City Bank and the great Standard Oil Company.

The business of the bank displayed new life almost immediately. In 1891 its deposits were only twelve million dollars, but before the end of the panic year 1893, they had risen to thirty-one millions. In 1891 there were several New York banks with double the deposits of the City Bank; two years later it was the largest bank in New York and was steadily becoming the greatest reservoir of cash in America. Slowly but surely the alliance with the Rockefeller interests became closer. William Rockefeller, who for many years had been in charge of the finances of Standard Oil, invested more and more of its surplus through the instrumentality of the City Bank. In the dark days of 1893, whenever the Standard Oil stepped into Wall Street to relieve the money strain by lending its idle millions temporarily, the City Bank handled the business. It was not long, therefore, before the institution began to be known as the "Standard Oil Bank."

But lending money in Wall Street was, indeed, only a small job for Standard Oil, whose cash assets grew, between 1882 and 1895, from $55,000,000 to over $150,000,000, while at the same time its stockholders received no less than $118,000,000 in dividends. This great accumulation of cash was not needed in the oil business, and it had to be put to some profitable use. The Rockefellers were not the type of investors who were satisfied with five or six per cent; they had been educated in a different school. They meant to make, if possible, as large profits in the investment of their surplus cash as they had been accustomed to make in their own line of business. But to make money at so rapid a pace called for the same shrewd, superior business methods that had been followed in the oil business. To discerning men, it was clear that ultimately these other enterprises into which Standard Oil put its funds must be controlled or dominated by Standard Oil. William Rockefeller had anticipated this development to some extent years before when he became active in the financial management of the Chicago, Milwaukee and St. Paul Railroad. But it was not until after the panic of 1893 that he and his associates began to reach out aggressively to control the destinies of many corporations.

When in 1897, Edward H. Harriman and Kuhn, Loeb and Company agreed upon the reorganization of the Union Pacific, as will be narrated in a subsequent chapter, they decided to finance the undertaking through the City Bank. They chose this bank because the Union Pacific reorganization, involving a payment of over $45,000,000 in cash to the United States Government, was then the largest cash transaction of its kind, and the City Bank, with its great name and resources, was the fittest instrument for their purpose. In this way Standard Oil became associated with the Union Pacific and with the Harriman and Kuhn-Loeb interests. Among the first directors of the reorganized Union Pacific were Jacob H. Schiff, Edward H. Harriman, Henry C. Frick, James Stillman, and William Rockefeller. The City Bank men did not at first put much money into the Union Pacific; but they were important factors in the underwriting syndicate, which got millions of stock as a fee. Many more millions were later bought by the members of the syndicate at from twenty to thirty dollars a share, until ultimately about one-third of the entire stock (practically the control) rested in the hands of William Rockefeller, James Stillman, Edward H. Harriman, and Kuhn, Loeb and Company.

From the very start the Union Pacific was financed in traditional Standard Oil fashion. It was a veritable bank. It kept and handled great cash resources with all the skill of the strong financiers who were charged with its management. In the following decade, through the brilliant and

daring activities of Harriman, with the solid backing of Standard Oil, the Union Pacific rolled up
nearly a billion and a half of capital on its own
system and held the absolute control of about
two billions of other capital.

Meanwhile the profits of Standard Oil, and of
the Rockefeller group as a whole, were rolling over
and over and growing like a snowball. The Union
Pacific alone was not enough to keep this great
money mill working. Other outlets must be found.
William Rockefeller increased his interest in the
St. Paul; John D. Rockefeller, whose only important activity outside of petroleum had been the
Lake Superior ore lands, now joined with the de-
cadent management of the Jay Gould estate, and
bought large investments in the New York, New
Haven and Hartford and other eastern railroad
systems. And still other activities engaged this
same group as the decade closed. The City Bank
— now the National City Bank — had tradition-
ally been the bank of the metal merchants and
had always kept its connections with them. There
were also men in the Standard Oil group who were
identified with raw materials, particularly copper. Henry H. Rogers, who was now vice-president of the Standard Oil Company and practically

its manager and who had in recent years gone extensively into copper mining, now formed a gigantic holding company known as the Amalgamated Copper Company, which acquired control of the Anaconda Copper Company at Butte, Montana. This syndicate was floated in Wall Street through the National City Bank. The capital was $150,000,000, and Amalgamated Copper, supported by Rockefeller money and the immense prestige of Standard Oil, at once became the favorite speculative stock of the day.

The deposits of the National City Bank had now mounted to above $100,000,000, and its capital had increased from a nominal three millions to twenty-five millions, with fifteen millions of surplus. It overshadowed every other institution in the country. The so-called Morgan banks, such as the First National, began to look like pygmies beside it. The bank now occupied a unique position in the eyes of the American public; it was the leading institution of the "Money Power." And by "Money Power" was usually meant the Rockefellers and their allies, who were constantly showing their influence and power in new directions. They had recently gone into public utilities, and jointly with William C. Whitney, who was allied by marriage with Oliver H. Payne and had become a large stockholder in Standard Oil, had secured control of the Consolidated Gas Company of New York. The latter company in turn had acquired control of several competing gas companies, hitherto identified with the old City Bank interests. Then in 1899 had occurred the spectacular merger with the Edison Illuminating Company of New York. By one stroke all the lighting companies in New York City were brought under one control. It looked as though the Morgan star was about to be eclipsed by a more powerful luminary.

CHAPTER V

THE STEEL TRUST MERGER

In this story of fabulous wealth and phenomenal prosperity we have almost lost sight of the disastrous panic of 1893, from which most of the large industrial enterprises of the United States emerged in a dilapidated condition. In the long depression which followed, manufacturers everywhere were forced into bankruptcy. Capital was scarce, the demand for goods was small, and thousands of plants remained in total or partial idleness for several years. This was particularly true of the steel and iron industry. Most of the steel plants, always excepting the Carnegie Works, were dormant or moribund. Dividends were discontinued; foreclosures were the order of the day; investors had lost their capital.

The tariff changes of 1894 had been a hard blow to many industries which had grown up and fattened in a quiet way during the long period of high protection from the close of the Civil War to the second Cleveland administration. Then, too, the Sherman Act of 1890, aimed particularly at combinations in restraint of trade, had frightened investors away from such "industrial trusts" as the Standard Oil Trust, the Cordage Trust, the Sugar Trust, and the Whiskey Trust which in the eighties had thrived, unmolested by the law. While they were all finally reorganized in such a way as to avoid the penalties of the law, banking and investment prejudice was strongly against them.

But when the Republican party returned to power in 1897 and immediately enacted a new tariff law, with high protective duties, and when at the same time certain court decisions were handed down which seemed to limit the scope of the Sherman Act, a wave of reviving prosperity swept over the country, and capital turned with new confidence to the industrial field. Several of the earlier trusts besides Standard Oil had survived the panic and had been reorganized to conform to the law, notably, the American Sugar Refining Company and the American Tobacco Company. The new industrial combinations were modeled after these. Instead of placing the control of acquired plants in the hands of "trustees,"

holding companies were formed, which acquired
all or a majority of stocks in certain competing
plants and merged these plants under one control,
often by exchanging the stock of the holding
company for the stock of the plant.

The industrial consolidation movement was aggressively under way by 1899, when the time for
it was ripe.   Money was cheap, credit was everywhere available, and prosperity was rising throughout the country.   All the important railroad reorganizations, as we have seen, had been carried
through, and the great bankers, whose coffers
swelled with huge underwriting commissions, were
looking for new business.   When the promoters of
the new type of industrial combination sought
banking support in Wall Street, they met with
little difficulty.   Wall Street was not slow to per-
ceive great possibilities in the financing of big industrial enterprises.   A conspicuous example was
the American Tobacco Company, which had been
created in 1890 as a combination of Allen and
Ginter of Richmond, W. Duke, Sons and Company
of Durham, North Carolina, and a number of other
well-known manufacturers.   Its original capital
had been ten millions of preferred stock, representing the cost of the properties, and fifteen millions

of common stock, representing good will or "water." But the business had forged ahead so rapidly that by 1898 the "capital" was multiplied fivefold, creating a new group of millionaires.

Then arose the great Amalgamated Copper Company, under the direction of Henry H. Rogers, and speculation in "industrials" became more and more the order of the day on the Stock Exchange. In quick succession a long string of new combinations followed; notably the American Smelting and Refining Company, with more than one hundred millions of capital and embracing over one hundred plants; the American Woolen Company, consolidating a large number of New England woolen mills under a fifty million dollar capitalization; the American Car and Foundry Company, merging the large car-building plants; the American Hide and Leather Company, consolidating over twenty large manufacturers of upper leathers; the International Paper Company, a fifty million dollar combination of paper manufacturers; and a large number of other similar mergers in various lines of industry.

But the biggest of all the industrial trusts was the merger of the steel and iron interests of the country, which began with the incorporation of the

Federal Steel Company in September, 1898, as a holding company to acquire the stocks of the Illinois Steel Company, the Minnesota Iron Company, the Lorain Steel Company, and the Elgin, Joliet and Eastern Railway, a belt line operating about the city of Chicago. The authorized capital of this new concern was two hundred million dollars, of which about one-half was issued at the start. It was a powerful combination and was in the hands of strong and able financiers. The firm of J. P. Morgan and Company took a leading part in financing the enterprise. The general counsel of the Illinois Steel Company, Judge Elbert H. Gary, a leading corporation lawyer of Chicago, thus came into close touch with "Jupiter" Morgan and was chosen as the first president of the new company. The wisdom of the choice was well demonstrated by subsequent experience.

Following came the American Steel and Wire Company, with ninety millions of capital, fathered by the well-known John W. Gates. This was a combination of big western plants, many of them specializing in barbed wire, nails, and wire fencing, but including many other industries and encroaching more or less closely on the field preëmpted by the Federal Steel Company. Gates had originally been a barbed wire salesman and was a notorious speculator. There followed still other companies: the American Tin Plate Company, with fifty millions of capital, the American Steel Hoop Company, the National Steel Company, and two Morgan consolidations, the National Tube Company and the American Bridge Company.

Carnegie and his associates were watching the situation closely. The great revival in steel and iron had naturally favored them, and their power was steadily growing. But Carnegie and his two chief partners, Frick and Phipps, viewed the empire of business from different angles. For a decade or more Carnegie had been genuinely anxious to retire. He had made his millions, he was getting on in life, and he had no desire to become a great banker with multitudinous outside interests, like Morgan, William Rockefeller, or Stillman. Henry C. Frick, on the other hand, was a natural master of capital; he foresaw the trend of the times. To his mind the days of one-man power were over; great enterprises in the future would be dominated and controlled by groups of capitalists of diverse interests; and even complete industries, if they hoped to live, would of necessity become allied with others. He believed that combination must take the place of competition and that he and his associates must sooner or later become a part of the consolidation movement. Carnegie saw in the movement only an opportunity to sell out at his own price. Naturally Carnegie and Frick quarreled. Frick was becoming more and more interested in matters outside of the steel business. He had been connected with William Rockefeller and Henry H. Rogers in various enterprises and was even then one of the largest stockholders in the Pennsylvania Railroad, a director in many corporations, and a conspicuous figure in Wall Street. These activities displeased Carnegie. His other partner, Henry Phipps, sided with Frick and so also estranged himself from Carnegie.

Meanwhile a group of Chicago speculators and promoters had come to the front. William H. Moore, a daring promoter, had organized the Diamond Match Company, the National Biscuit Company, and the American Tin Plate Company. He and his associates had made several millions out of the organization of the American Steel Hoop Company and the National Steel Company. Flushed with success and with big cash balances, Moore now approached Carnegie and offered him a million dollars for a ninety-day option on his stock in the Carnegie Steel Company, the price being $157,950,000 of which over a third was to be in cash. Carnegie agreed, provided Moore would take Frick and Phipps with him. Carnegie guessed that while Moore single handed might not be able to raise the money, Frick, Phipps, and Moore together surely would. But it was not all plain sailing. Morgan had not yet become convinced of the soundness of the industrial movement; the Rockefellers could not be made to see the possibilities of such a gigantic scheme as this, though John D. Rockefeller had personally taken some interest in the Federal Steel Company. And just then a temporary panic occurred in Wall Street, as a result of the sudden death of Roswell P. Flower, who had been the conspicuous operator in the inflated bull market. This incident hampered the efforts of Frick and Moore and before they could raise the necessary money the ninety-day option had expired. Carnegie refused to extend it a single day and quietly pocketed the million dollars which had been given him for the option.

As the steel business continued to flourish and the country enjoyed great prosperity, Carnegie decided that his first offer had been entirely too cheap, and a little later, when John D. Rockefeller tried to buy him out, he placed his price at $250,000,000. It was Rockefeller's desire to solidify his interests in the ore lands and ore railway in Minnesota, as well as the capital invested in his fleet of ore-carrying vessels on the Great Lakes. But Carnegie's price was too high for Rockefeller, and nothing came of the proposal.

When Andrew Carnegie was laying the foundations of his steel and iron business, he built a small summer bungalow at Cresson Springs, Pennsylvania. Here there was a livery stable run by a man named Schwab, from whom Carnegie was in the habit of hiring horses. Schwab had a son called Charlie who used to hang around the livery stable, a merry, good-natured youngster whom every one liked. The boy had a good voice and interested Carnegie, who was very fond of music. "When that boy of yours is ready for a job, send him to me," said Carnegie to the father one day.

And so, by good luck, in 1880, at the age of eighteen, Charles M. Schwab entered the employment of Carnegie in the Edgar Thomson Steel Works. The young fellow made good and became chief engineer and assistant manager. When Carnegie bought out an important competitor at Homestead, Schwab was selected as superintendent of the plant and showed his mettle by promptly making the Homestead Steel Works the most profitable of all the Carnegie properties. In 1889 he was brought back to Braddock and placed in charge of the Edgar Thomson Steel Works and three years later was made general superintendent of both plants.

Some time afterward Carnegie told Schwab that he had decided to make him a vice-president, to which Schwab replied:

"No, Mr. Carnegie, I am no good carrying out other men's orders, and I should have to do that as a vice-president. As superintendent I am boss of the plants I manage."

Later again Carnegie approached him. "Well," he said, "if you won't be vice-president, I suppose we'll have to make you president." And they did. In 1897 Charles M. Schwab became president of the Carnegie Steel Company.

Schwab naturally adopted Carnegie's ideas and business policy. He was long opposed to Frick's theory that the future of successful business lay in combination and interdependence. "A big business enterprise," he said, "is invariably built up around one man." But this was simply an echo of the philosophy of Carnegie, and when the "community of interest" movement began to dominate American industry Schwab gradually changed his view. He was but thirty-eight years old, and his life was still before him. Carnegie at sixty-five was naturally wedded to the theories of the old school. Besides, Carnegie wanted to retire from business, while Schwab felt that he was just getting into business. At a banquet given to him at the University Club in New York, the younger man came out strongly in favor of combination among corporations and deprecated cutthroat competition and the rule-or-ruin policy.

After the failure of the negotiations with Moore and Rockefeller for the sale of his business, Carnegie quietly bided his time until the Morgan interests had plunged so deeply into the steel business in connection with the Federal Steel Company, the National Tube Company, and the American Bridge Company, that they could not possibly back out. Then he set on foot a series of operations designed to create havoc among all the steel corporations of the country. To fight Morgan he announced that he would go into the tube business in direct competition with the National Tube

Company, and he actually acquired five thousand acres of land at Conneaut on Lake Erie and let contracts for the construction of a twelve million dollar tube plant.   To fight John W. Gates and his American Steel and Wire Company, he announced that a gigantic rod-mill would be erected at Pittsburgh. To fight Rockefeller, he ordered the construction of a large fleet of ore-carrying steamships to operate on the Great Lakes.   To fight the Pennsylvania Railroad, he set a corps of surveyors laying out a railroad route from Pittsburgh to the Atlantic Ocean.   He also planned the immediate construction of an ore-carrying railroad of vast capacity from Lake Erie to the Pittsburgh district.

Such threats as these were taken seriously, for everybody recognized that Carnegie had the power to carry them through.   Already he had the whip hand in the steel world.   The profits of his corporation in 1900 had been over forty million dollars; he was already making over one-fourth of the Bessemer steel produced in the country and half of the structural steel and armor plate.   His costs were lower than those of any of his competitors, and he had no debts.   The entire steel trade of the country was thrown into confusion.   There was an actual panic among the millionaires of Wall Street.

"We must get rid of Carnegie," they all shouted. "He will wreck both himself and us; he is a business pirate." And the frightened financiers, whose millions were tied up in Federal Steel, American Steel and Wire, and the other great companies, rushed to Morgan for help. The Standard Oil bankers were appealed to; but the undertaking called for such a gigantic outlay and was fraught with such uncertainties, that even these bold financiers hesitated, evidently preferring that Morgan should bear the brunt of the responsibility.

Just at this time, Charles M. Schwab and John W. Gates put their heads together and agreed to interview Morgan. Whether Schwab's overtures were directed by Carnegie or not may never be known, but Schwab by this time saw as clearly as any one that interdependence in the steel business was absolutely essential to its future prosperity. As for Gates, his motives were clear enough: he was one of the panic-stricken millionaires who were threatened with disaster. Schwab and Gates spent eight hours trying to convince Morgan of the necessity of buying Carnegie out. Schwab set forth the strong features of the Carnegie business and the glittering possibilities of industrial peace by means of a combination. Tradition says that he spoke with much eloquence; at any rate he made the sale; Morgan agreed to pay Carnegie his price. This price was much higher than that stated to Frick and Moore only eighteen months before, higher even than the price named to John D. Rockefeller the previous year. Frick and Moore could have bought the entire Carnegie business for about $157,000,000; it was offered to Rockefeller for $250,000,000; but the amount Morgan paid in January, 1901, was equivalent to a cash price of over $447,000,000. This was represented by giving Carnegie and his associates $303,450,000 in bonds and nearly two hundred million dollars' worth of stock which immediately had a market value of about $144,000,000. It was the greatest sale in the history of the world.

Carnegie was now definitely shelved, so far as the steel business was concerned; his tube plant scheme at Conneaut, his plans for a railroad from Pittsburgh to the sea, and his big rod-mill project at Pittsburgh were all abandoned. But Morgan found his hands full when he came to deal with the other big steel interests. The Federal Steel directors, aside from Judge Gary, had opposed the idea of allowing Carnegie to sandbag them; Gates now felt that Morgan should pay him a bigger price for American Steel and Wire than he had first named; Rockefeller, with his rich Lake Superior ore beds, also wanted large concessions if he was to become a party to the combination. In short, all the companies which it was planned to put into the merger suddenly discovered that their properties were worth millions more, now that the menace of Carnegie had been removed.

It was indeed a difficult task that confronted Pierpont Morgan. The various smaller steel "trusts" that had been formed during the two previous years were overcapitalized and had issued reams of "watered" stocks. For when the mania for consolidation was under full swing during the period which began with the close of the war with Spain in 1898, discretion had been thrown to the winds, and industrial plants of every type had been bought up by promoters regardless of price. An incident is told which — whether true or not — will illustrate the tendency. When one of the smaller "trusts" was being formed, a party of steel men were on their way to Chicago one night after a buying tour. The men had been drinking and were in a convivial mood. Said one, "There's a steel mill at the next station; let's get out and buy it." "Agreed!"

It was past midnight when they reached the

station, but they pulled the plant owner out of bed and demanded that he sell his plant.

"My plant is worth two hundred thousand dollars, but it is not for sale," was the reply.

"Never mind about the price," answered the hilarious purchasers, "we will give you three hundred thousand — five hundred thousand."

The story is not improbable, for most of the constituent plants had been bought at prices far above their true values. Consequently, the corporation to be formed must have a fabulous capitalization; and stocks and bonds must be issued many times in excess of what the properties would have brought at forced sales in normal times. But Pierpont Morgan was equal to the emergency. He first called in his big lieutenants, one of whom was his young partner, George W. Perkins — a man destined to influence profoundly the policy and fortunes of the corporation about to be born — and the magnates of the independent companies, including Elbert H. Gary, Marshall Field, Norman B. Ream, Henry C. Frick, and H. H. Rogers. It was Morgan's plan at first to include in the combination only those steel companies with which his firm had already become identified, but it was soon seen that it would be dangerous to exclude the others. If the Gates interests were left out, they might become a menace to the peace of the new concern, for John W. Gates would surely attempt to sandbag Morgan as Carnegie had done. If the Moore brothers were left to shift for themselves, they might get together with others and do the same thing. The chief danger was, however, from the Standard Oil. To allow John D. Rockefeller to remain independent, with his big Lake Superior deposits and his fleet of ore-carrying vessels on the Lake, might easily lead to disaster. A second monster steel business might easily be built up under Standard Oil control. Therefore it must be a case of all or none. The steel industry must be completely merged into one, and all companies of strong financial connections or large resources must be included.

Judge Gary was appointed to open up negotiations with the independents. Daniel G. Reid, of the American Steel Hoop Company, was brought in, and he induced the Moore brothers to join the combination. The Gates group received what they demanded, and then Henry C. Frick was sent to see what he could do with John D. Rockefeller. Frick's position at this time was somewhat unique. Since his break with Carnegie a couple of

years before he had become more of a Wall Street
speculator than a mere steel man. He had not
definitely allied himself with either Morgan or
Rockefeller but was on friendly terms with both.
He had close associations with Henry H. Rogers
and James Stillman; he had gone into Federal Steel;
he was a powerful factor in the affairs of the Pennsylvania Railroad; altogether, he was looked upon
as one of the leading protagonists of the "community of interest" idea which had been so strongly
championed by Cassatt of the Pennsylvania Railroad, Harriman of the Union Pacific, and Hill of
the Great Northern.

Frick succeeded without much trouble in bag-
ging Rockefeller, although the price he paid looked
high at the time.   Rockefeller received eighty millions in the stock of the new corporation, of which
half was preferred stock, besides eight and one-
half million dollars in cash for his ore-carrying
fleet. These were huge concessions, but the control
of the Lake Superior iron mines was absolutely
essential, for these deposits represented two-thirds
of the new corporation's ore supply.

Having thus gathered together all the important
steel interests of the country, Morgan launched
the United States Steel Corporation. The stock

capitalization was in excess of a billion dollars, with a bonded debt of more than three hundred millions, and both the big banking groups of Wall Street were firmly tied to the enterprise. The great merger dominated by Morgan drew into its orbit even the Standard Oil "Money Power." Among the big names included in the syndicate, aside from Morgan and his partners, were H. H. Rogers and Daniel O'Day of Standard Oil; Marshall Field, William H. Moore, James H. Moore, Elbert H. Gary, John W. Gates, H. H. Porter, and Norman B. Ream, of Chicago; Samuel Mather of Cleveland; Nathaniel Thayer of Boston; and Daniel G. Reid, Henry C. Frick, Charles M. Schwab, and D. O. Mills, of New York. So under the control of a single corporation passed seventy per cent of the American iron and steel industry. That industry, instead of being operated on the old plan of individual control or independent corporate control, was now linked with scores of banks of great power, with railroads, and with numerous other corporate undertakings.

CHAPTER VI

EDWARD H. HARRIMAN was the son of a poor and unsuccessful Episcopal clergyman who spent the latter days of his life as a bookkeeper in the old Bank of Commerce in New York. Born in 1848, young Harriman was just fourteen years old when his father obtained a job for him as office boy with DeWitt C. Hays, a Wall Street stockbroker. This was just about the time when Pierpont Morgan was preparing to get into business in America; when Andrew Carnegie was accumulating his first money in speculative oil and railroad ventures under the tutelage of Scott and was scanning the horizon of the new Bessemer steel business; when John D. Rockefeller was laying the foundations of Standard Oil; and when Henry C. Frick — one year younger than Harriman — was doing duty as an errand boy in Mount Pleasant.

From the very first, young Harriman displayed

unusual ability. He also had that trait of audacity which had shown so conspicuously in the characters of Frick, Carnegie, and Morgan. Almost immediately he began to make a little money in stocks. And he widened his acquaintance rapidly. He became intimate with Lewis Livingston, a member of one of the oldest New York families, who had a son named James. When in 1870, after having worked himself up to the position of bookkeeper of the Hays firm, young Harriman bought a seat in the New York Stock Exchange at a cost of about three thousand dollars, he induced James Livingston to go into the stock brokerage business with him and supply capital through his father. Harriman was successful at once — so successful that within a few months he dissolved partnership with Livingston and formed a new firm with himself at the head and his brother William as a partner. He cultivated the friendship of people of means and social standing and in a few years became prominent among the younger "aristocrats" of New York. In this environment he ultimately came into close touch with the people associated with the Illinois Central Railroad, which had been built during the years prior to the Civil War and had proved wonderfully successful from the start

Running north and south, it caught broadside the westbound tide of migration; its government grant of rich Mississippi Valley lands was sold early at a good price; soon after it was built the Civil War gave it a big business, and it escaped the ruinous competition which so long devastated the trunk lines running east and west.

A group of old New York merchants had built this road. Though they sold five-sixths of its stock in England and Holland, it became a favorite solid investment for many of the old families of New York. The Astors and the Goelets and the Cuttings were large holders of its stock in the seventies and eighties. The Illinois Central, indeed, was quite the "society railroad" of New York. During the long period from 1857 to 1883 the property had remained under the direct control and operation of William Henry Osborne, an old Manila merchant who had returned from the Philippines in the fifties with a fortune and who had operated the Illinois Central all these years as he would have operated his own warehouse. Osborne had a summer home at Garrison, New York, where he was a neighbor of the old and rich Fish family, a younger member of which was Stuyvesant Fish. The latter became Osborne's secretary in 1872 and a few years later was made a director of the railroad. In 1883 when Osborne died, he practically bequeathed the management of the railroad to his secretary, although Fish did not actually become president until some years later.

Harriman and Fish had known each other for many years, and as young men had traveled about town a great deal together. In 1880 they were both directors in the Ogdensburg and Lake Champlain Railroad, a property of which Harriman had hoped to acquire the control, for by this time Harriman had made very substantial progress in business, having accumulated several hundred thousand dollars through shrewd trading in securities. He was now beginning to turn away from mere brokerage to railroad management and finance.

The Illinois Central had acquired control of an extensive system of lines south of St. Louis, known as the Chicago, St. Louis and New Orleans, and Stuyvesant Fish had sought Harriman's assistance in placing the bonds. In this work Harriman was notably successful. Meanwhile he had himself acquired a large block of Illinois Central stock and had become more and more the confidential adviser of Fish. At that time there was a large Dutch stockholding interest in the road, whose

votes were cast collectively by the firm that had
originally placed the stock in Holland, Boissevain
Brothers.   One member of this firm came on a visit
to America.   Harriman met him, gained his confidence, and then arranged to hold his proxies in the
Illinois Central meetings.   Soon afterwards Harriman was elected a director and became the close
associate of Stuyvesant Fish in the actual operation
and control of the road.

No two men could have been more dissimilar in
personality and bearing than these two.   Harriman was small, quiet, restless, and secretive; Fish
was a big, open-faced, easy-mannered young man,
whose blond hair and great stature had earned for
him in the financial district the name of "White
Elephant."   For a time, however, the two men
worked together in harmony.   They bought a portion of the old Wabash, St. Louis and Pacific after
its failure in 1884; in 1887 they bought the Dubuque and Sioux City Railroad; in the early nineties they bought (much against the will of Collis P.
Huntington) the chain of roads with which Huntington had planned to hitch his Southern Pacific
system to the Atlantic seaboard; they bought an
important section of the St. Louis, Alton and Terre
Haute, which George Foster Peabody had been

developing in southern Illinois, thus securing an entry of their own into St. Louis; and they purchased a great number of small roads, until, from the two thousand miles they had in 1883, they owned and controlled in 1897 a system of over five thousand miles.

This policy of expansion did not bring disaster, as had been the case with so many other lines. All through this period the road's credit remained high, and even in the early eighties it was able to sell three and one-half per cent bonds while other roads of good credit were raising money at five or six per cent. This high credit of the Illinois Central was very largely due to the rigid policies which Harriman introduced and developed. Harriman was more than a mere banker or broker; he was a practical railroad operating man. He had made a thorough study of railroading and had early adopted the theory that the first duty of railroad management was to maintain the character of the physical property and to consider mere current profits as secondary. Thus, in the management of the Illinois Central, he never "skinned" the road to pay dividends; he never allowed the roadbed or equipment to become inefficient. Another sound idea he adopted was always to provide ample funds and reserves for contingencies; never to allow his property to take financial chances in times of dullness or depression. Even when he was raising large amounts of new capital for extensions or purchases, he always provided far more cash assets than were currently needed.

Harriman had very soon grown powerful enough to cross the path of Pierpont Morgan. In 1887, Morgan held the proxies of the stockholders in the Dubuque and Sioux City Railroad, which Harriman wished to buy for the Illinois Central. Harriman fought his plan through and defeated Morgan. This coup was regarded as a ten days' wonder in Wall Street. From that time on Morgan disliked Harriman. Again, in 1894, Harriman and Morgan crossed swords. Harriman owned a few hundred thousand dollars worth of underlying bonds about the time that Morgan announced his plan of reorganization for the Erie Railroad. Harriman objected to the proposed treatment of his securities, brought suit to prevent the drastic reorganization, and in the end forced Morgan to make concessions.

Harriman was as yet little known outside of Wall Street. Although chairman of the finance committee of the Illinois Central and the power behind the throne, he was eclipsed by the figure of

Fish. But in 1895 Harriman stepped to the front. The Union Pacific Railroad security holders were looking in vain for some strong banking interests to finance their property. The road was a frightful wreck with a tangled mass of subsidiary companies, and the United States Government was aggressively insisting on the payment of the huge debt representing the original government loans, with the interest that had accumulated since its building thirty years before. Morgan had rejected the suggestion that he reorganize it, as he was too fully occupied with the rejuvenation of many other railroad systems. Harriman then saw his chance. He decided to reorganize the Union Pacific himself, to make it a subsidiary of the Illinois Central, and to utilize the credit of the latter company for the gigantic financing which would be necessary. But before he had progressed very far in this plan he met with opposition from Kuhn, Loeb and Company, who had become bankers for the Chicago, Milwaukee and St. Paul, the Great Northern Railway, and other properties, and now also were bent upon reorganizing the Union Pacific.

A keen contest for mastery followed. At first Jacob H. Schiff, the head of Kuhn, Loeb and Company, persistently ignored Harriman, feeling confident that no interest in New York could successfully reorganize the property except Morgan or himself; but Harriman soon forced him to change his mind. The two were brought together, and, in Wall Street parlance, laid their respective cards on the table. It was an interesting and convincing show-down. Schiff could raise the much needed hundred millions of new capital at five or six per cent through his strong German connections; but Harriman showed how he could raise this sum, and more, on the Illinois Central credit, at from three and one-half to four per cent. Schiff capitulated, and finally reached an agreement with this new master of capital. The road was reorganized by Kuhn, Loeb and Company, and Edward H. Harriman was made the first chairman of its board of directors and later its president.

Harriman had now leaped at a bound into public notice. And, coincidently, as we have already seen — an event of great significance — the powerful Standard Oil capitalists interested themselves in Wall Street affairs.

Too much credit cannot be given to the men who carried out this reorganization of the Union Pacific Railroad. In the first place, they paid to the

Federal Government over forty-five million dollars in cash on a bankrupt railroad — all the principal and full interest at six per cent on the Union Pacific debt, which had accrued for thirty years. Then they put the bonds and preferred stock of the reorganized road on a straight four per cent basis; and finally after these prudential measures, they began to spend money by the tens and hundreds of millions upon this ramshackle property running across the "Great American Desert."

In all these operations Harriman was the masterful leader. Fortune played into his hands. For the first time in years the arid farming sections of the West had copious rains and fine crops. The Spanish-American War resulted in American occupation of the Philippines; and the Union Pacific got a great business from these new possessions. Harriman not only spent money but he spent it quickly, accomplishing in two years' work what had been estimated to take five. And he was reaping the fruit of his enterprise. In three years, under his direction, the system expanded from less than two thousand miles to over fifteen thousand. The old branches running up into the Oregon country were all reabsorbed. After the death of Collis P. Huntington in 1900, Harriman bought in forty-five per cent of the Southern Pacific Company stock, principally from the Huntington estate.

But now, just about the time that the great steel merger was being carried through, when the big banking interests of Wall Street were everywhere hitching themselves to the Morgan star, Harriman's gigantic railroad plans came into violent collision with the equally gigantic plans of James J. Hill. Until a short time before this, Hill had not been looked upon as a big operator in Wall Street. He had won fame as the builder and successful manager of the Great Northern Railway system, but he had not been directly involved in the large Wall Street deals. At first, as the Great Northern emerged from the panic of 1893, the firm of Kuhn, Loeb and Company had done most of the Great Northern financing in New York. But after the reorganization of the Northern Pacific property by Morgan in 1897, Hill and Morgan began to work closer to each other. Hill had acquired a substantial stock interest in the Chase National Bank, one of New York City's old and strong institutions, while Morgan began to add to his interest in the First National Bank, of which George F. Baker was president. Baker and his associates at this time also acquired a large interest in the Chase National Bank, and the two institutions became definitely allied in interest. Then, as a natural step, James J. Hill acquired an important interest in the First National Bank. A little later, Hill acquired a large part of the Morgan interest in the newly reorganized Northern Pacific property. This move brought Hill definitely into the group of Morgan financiers, while Harriman was still closely associated with the Rockefeller and City Bank interests.

Hill was now the controlling power in both the Great Northern and the Northern Pacific systems and was becoming more and more of a competitor of Harriman. The latter discerned the dangers ahead and began to extend the Union Pacific branch lines up into the Oregon district. But Hill was looking to the East. Neither of his roads controlled a connection to Chicago, the Northern Pacific ending at St. Paul, and the Great Northern at Duluth. The Union Pacific, on the other hand, had a close alliance with the Illinois Central, which entered Chicago, and maintained traffic connections with other lines. At this juncture Hill decided to have the Northern Pacific buy the stock control of the great Chicago, Burlington and Quincy system. When this move was announced, it threw the Harriman people into confusion, for it meant that the Union Pacific would have a direct competitor a third of the way to the Pacific. While the Burlington line was bought primarily for the sake of its lines extending from St. Paul southward to Chicago, yet the system had also a lucrative line running to Denver and far beyond into Wyoming.

Harriman now attempted to bargain with Hill and to induce him to let the Union Pacific join in the Burlington purchase and thus tie up all the western systems in a common monopoly. But Hill refused. Then, without the slightest hesitation, Harriman quietly began to buy up the control of the Northern Pacific in the open stock market. In this way he hoped to checkmate Hill, as the Northern Pacific (jointly with the Great Northern) had been made the instrument to carry the Burlington stock and Harriman reasoned that, while a majority of Great Northern stock was doubtless locked up in the strong boxes of Hill and his friends, only a substantial minority of the Northern Pacific stock was so held.

To buy up the control of such a property meant the use of anywhere from $80,000,000 to $100,000,-000 in cash. But Harriman knew where he could lay his hands on the money. Already the Union Pacific had a heavy balance in its treasury; it had, besides, about $60,000,000 of unused bonds which Harriman had the right to issue; and behind him were the huge cash resources of Kuhn, Loeb and Company and the City Bank, with the Standard Oil alliance.

Harriman had gone far on the way to controlling the Northern Pacific before the fact was known to J. P. Morgan and Company. Morgan had gone on his usual spring and summer trip to Europe, and was on the ocean when the storm broke. Coster, his chief lieutenant, had died the year before. The Morgan firm was in charge of Robert Bacon, a fine, upstanding young man, handsome as a Greek god, but not of the Morgan caliber. He had been called to the Morgan firm a few years before from a brokerage house in Boston; but he was not the best substitute for Pierpont Morgan in a great financial crisis.

On the 1st of April, 1901, Morgan and the Hill people together held between $35,000,000 and $40,000,000 of the Northern Pacific stock out of a total of $155,000,000. They had paid an average of about sixteen for this stock only two or three years before and, seeing it rise beyond par, they were tempted to sell some of their holdings. On the 1st of May they held only $26,000,000 worth. Then Harriman announced that he had bought an actual majority of the Northern Pacific stock. And he had; but there was a loophole which Harriman had overlooked. His purchases were in both common and preferred stock, but the charter of the company provided that the preferred stock could be retired at the will of the directors, thus leaving the voting power entirely in the common stock. It soon appeared that Harriman had not acquired enough common stock to give him control. So Hill and his friends, with the Morgan house and its powerful connections, rallied and employed James R. Keene, the famous stock market manipulator, to buy a majority of the Northern Pacific stock for them. Between the 3d and the 7th of May over $15,000,000 worth was bought — enough, they thought, to give them an actual majority.

But at the same time Harriman also was buying; and by the 9th of May both parties claimed to have a majority. The stock had been "cornered"; the price soared and soared; at ten o'clock on the 9th of May it sold around $350 a share; one hour later it was quoted at $1000 a share. Wall

Street plunged into a panic; stocks of every character dropped with a thud; it was plain that, unless something was done, every broker and every banker in Wall Street would fail by nightfall. So the two contestants had to suspend hostilities in order to save the financial world they lived in. A truce was signed pending Morgan's return to New York in July. In November, Bacon retired, broken in health by the gigantic strain of the Morgan business, just as Coster before him had been. But his place was more than filled by George W. Perkins.

In the formation of the Northern Securities Company in the fall of 1901, another important link was forged which served to weld the rival financial groups of Wall Street together. The Northern Securities Company was a holding corporation with $400,000,000 capital, which was formed to acquire by exchange of stock all the capital of the Northern Pacific Railway and a majority of the capital of the Great Northern, thus insuring control of the Burlington, nearly all the stock of which had been acquired by these companies. As the Union Pacific and Harriman and Standard Oil interests had bought a great block of Northern Pacific stock, this agreement meant that they would control substantially half of the Northern Securities Company

stock.   Thus, by a gigantic stroke, railway competition in the vast region west of the Mississippi
was eliminated, and a combination of capital,
far greater than that of the Steel Trust, was
formed.   The Harriman properties now embraced
the Southern Pacific system, with its eleven thousand miles of railroad radiating throughout the
entire Southwest, and the Illinois Central, with its
five thousand miles extending down the Mississippi Valley to the Gulf.   The Hill properties, now
jointly controlled and operated by Hill and Harriman, included over fifteen thousand miles of lines
radiating throughout the entire rich region north
and northwest of Chicago and extending through
to the Pacific by two distinct routes.

But this alliance of western properties by no
means represented all or nearly all the railroad
power of either Harriman or Morgan.   Harriman
had caused the Union Pacific to acquire important
interests in the New York Central, the St. Paul,
the Atchison, and the Chicago and North-Western,
following out the "community of interest" theory
of which he was such a strong advocate.   Morgan,
on his part, was just as firmly as ever in control of
his eastern properties, the Erie and the Southern,
and had important influence in the management of

the Reading, the Lehigh Valley, the Baltimore and
Ohio and, of course, the entire Vanderbilt lines.
Interlocking directorates were becoming the vogue
in the entire railroad world. The powerful Pennsylvania Railroad, under the remarkable and force-
ful personality of Alexander J. Cassatt, had pushed
the "community of interest" idea aggressively,
and its representatives were on the boards of directors of all of its competing and many of its connecting lines. In nearly all directions, the railroad systems of the country had now been welded
together under the financial control of practically
one powerful interest.

There was, however, one loophole left open. The
lucrative Louisville and Nashville Railroad was
still outside the breastworks, when John W. Gates
— who, since he had sold out his American Steel
and Wire Company to the Trust in 1901, had become a notorious stock-market "plunger" — and
Edwin Hawley joined forces in 1903 and bought
a majority of the Louisville and Nashville stock.
Hawley had been one of the lieutenants of Collis
P. Huntington, after whose death and the sale
of the Southern Pacific to Harriman he had become a free lance. He bought small railroads for
the purpose of selling them out at a profit, just as a

smaller man would buy a block of stock for the same purpose. He and Gates formed a strong combination; but their reputation was that of manipulators; and it was feared that they would wreck the solid old Louisville and Nashville property in short order by unsound financing and unprincipled manipulation. In fact, this was their intention. They worked up an enormous speculation in the stock, caught certain large insiders short, and threatened to start another "corner" similar to that in the Northern Pacific. To prevent the recurrence of such a disaster, Morgan stepped in and took the Louisville and Nashville off their hands at their own price. Later, Morgan turned the control of this railroad property over to the Atlantic Coast Line, which had been welded together by Henry Walters and was being operated in harmony with the Morgan interests along the South Atlantic seaboard.

There was now but one large system of American railroads that actually escaped the control of conservative bankers of the Morgan and Standard Oil type, with their "community of interest" formula. This was the Chicago, Rock Island and Pacific. In 1902, their pockets bulging with the millions acquired in the big steel merger, the Moore brothers, with Daniel G. Reid, and others, formed a syndicate and bought the control of this property. They immediately loaded it up with several hundred millions of watered capital, and then so fixed the voting power that they could sell practically all of it to the public and yet still retain control of the property. Thus, the Rock Island system became simply a football for Wall Street gamblers; its roadbed and rolling stock were neglected; the road was "skinned" year after year to pay dividends; and an extravagant policy of expansion was pursued which in the course of time forced the entire system into bankruptcy, and the flimsy structure collapsed like a house of cards.

CHAPTER VII

IN 1903 the United Steel Corporation failed to earn
its dividends, its great issue of common stock fell
to a few dollars a share, and people began to think
that Morgan was no wizard after all. Carnegie,
the retired and intrenched multimillionaire, sat
back and laughed; Harriman, the enemy of Morgan, gloated over the fall of his rival; the Standard
Oil magnates, always jealous of the Morgan power,
said little but watched and waited. But while the
fickle public cried calamity, Morgan kept on being
a "bull." He knew that the ebb was temporary;
that the tide would soon turn. He urged his clients
to buy steel and other good industrials. The decision of the Supreme Court in 1904 ordering the
dissolution of the Northern Securities Company
caused a shiver in the framework of Morgan's gigantic structure. But it was only a shiver. The
tide did turn, and big business went merrily on

until the storm broke in 1907. Steel stocks rose above their original figures, and the house of Morgan regained its prestige and added to its financial strength.

During these years Morgan formed the great shipping combination known as the International Mercantile Marine Company, which absorbed the White Star Line, the American Line, the Red Star Line, the Leyland Line, and many other transatlantic companies. The idea of this combination was to eliminate the cutthroat competition which then existed in the transatlantic trade in freight and passenger rates. The leading lines between New York and England, which included the Cunard Line, the White Star, and the American Line, had suffered during the few previous years through competitive conditions just as the trunk line railroads had suffered for more than a decade prior to the period when the Morgan idea of "combinations" and "community of interest" had been so widely introduced. It was felt that the same methods of combination in the ocean carrying trade might have equally beneficial results.

But the organization of the International Mercantile Marine Company proved to be one of Morgan's business mistakes — until the unprecedented

demand for shipping in the World War resulted
in large earnings. The vital fact was apparently
belittled or overlooked that a combination of carriers on the high seas cannot be welded into a
monopoly in the same way that a combination of
railroads can be. The ocean is free to all comers,
while a railway right of way is in its very nature
exclusive and grows more valuable as the territory covered increases in density of population and
wealth. It would be practically impossible, because of the stupendous costs, for a direct competitor to be built today paralleling the Pennsylvania
Railroad between New York and Pittsburgh; but
it would be simple enough for an organization of
capital to establish an entirely new line of steamships between New York and Liverpool.

This was but one of the facts which were overlooked by the promoters of the steamship combination. The competing lines controlled in England
and Germany were all the beneficiaries of large
government subsidies, whereas the new Morgan
combination, being under American control and
financed by American capital, could not enjoy
these benefits. Moreover, as soon as the new
combination began to compete aggressively with
the Cunard and German lines, both the English

and German Governments came to the rescue with further large subsidies and benefits. The Cunard Line was able to make an arrangement with the British Government whereby the latter advanced money at two and one-half per cent for the construction of new liners of mammoth capacity, such as the *Lusitania* and the *Mauretania*.

A more successful flotation by the Morgan firm was that of the International Harvester Company. This was a gigantic combination of manufacturers of harvesting machinery and included the larger plants in the United States and also many of those in Europe. Its capitalization was large, but it distinctly stabilized business conditions in this line of industry and prospered notably from the very start. Credit was especially due to George W. Perkins, Morgan's young partner, for forming this new combination.

During a long period the Morgan firm had been closely identified with the General Electric Company, a great manufacturing concern which had been building up a world-wide industry. But the General Electric Company was now becoming more than a mere manufacturing concern. With its large capital and high credit it was steadily going into the business of developing public utility

operating companies. The old North American
Company, which had originated as the Oregon
and Transcontinental Company many years before
and had been the holding corporation for the interests of Henry Villard in connection with the
Northern Pacific and certain Oregon railways, had
now been revamped as a public utility holding
company and had gradually acquired control of,
or large interests in the street railways and light-
ing companies of St. Louis, the Milwaukee public
utilities, and the Detroit Edison Company.

But perhaps the most striking development of
this time was the further unification of railroad
control. After the Supreme Court decision dis-
solving the Northern Securities Company was
handed down in 1904, the stocks of the Great
Northern and Northern Pacific railways which
had been acquired by this holding company were
returned to their holders. The Union Pacific
Railway received into its treasury an enormous
amount of both Great Northern and Northern
Pacific stock. At this time, these stocks were of
tremendous market value. Both roads showed
large earnings and were paying liberal dividends, besides cutting "melons" by dividing surplus profits in one form or another. The stock market was

booming, and the quotations in these stocks soared to unheard-of heights. Great Northern stock sold in 1906 as high as $340 a share and Northern Pacific at about $230. The Union Pacific suddenly found itself rich beyond the dreams of avarice; its treasury was overflowing with valuable securities. And when, after this dissolution, the Harriman and Hill interests reached a definite agreement on matters of policy and division of territory by carrying the "community of interest" idea to its logical conclusion, there was no further need of the Union Pacific to retain control of these large amounts of stock. So Harriman decided to dispose of them. These sales, which were spread over a considerable period, brought an immense amount of cash into the treasury of the company and resulted in a total profit to the Union Pacific of more than fifty millions of dollars.

Thus the Union Pacific Railway had become a veritable storehouse of cash, in fact, a bank of enormous resources. But Harriman had no intention of allowing the railroad to remain a bank; he had more ambitious plans. The Supreme Court decision, while preventing the practical merger of competing lines, said nothing about the control of connecting lines. So the Union Pacific cash was immediately employed in adding to the Union Pacific's interest in connecting systems. It had always been Harriman's ambition to control an ocean to ocean railroad, and he now began to purchase in the interest of the Union Pacific great blocks of stock in the Baltimore and Ohio Railroad, besides adding heavily to that already owned by the Union Pacific in the Illinois Central. By the early part of 1906, the Baltimore and Ohio was practically an eastern arm of the Union Pacific Railway. And inasmuch as the Baltimore and Ohio already owned practically a dominating interest in the Reading Company, with the control of the anthracite fields, and the Reading controlled the Central Railroad of New Jersey, with its entrance into the New York City district, the Union Pacific now became a network of railway lines extending from ocean to ocean.

In short, the general tendency was for all the American railroads to become more and more closely knit together in policy and interest. The St. Paul in these years began to develop its western extension, and the Rockefeller interests, which were so closely allied with the Harriman railroad financiers, had complete control of the St. Paul. The Gould properties were being linked into one harmonious whole, and a plan was under way for a Gould transcontinental line also stretching from ocean to ocean. The Western Maryland system was acquired by the Goulds, with Rockefeller aid, and it looked as though a great system would soon be built up, side by side with the Harriman lines, but in close control and with the maintenance of harmonious relations.

The Hill and Morgan properties of course exhibited this same tendency towards greater harmony and concentration. Hill's lines radiated throughout the Northwest but worked in harmony with both the Harriman and the Rockefeller interests. The Atlantic Coast Line, with the great Louisville and Nashville system, under the management of Henry Walters and under the partial control of Morgan interests, operated in complete harmony with the Southern Railway system on the one hand and with the Illinois Central on the other. Morgan took care that his Erie system maintained favorable and harmonious relations with the great Vanderbilt lines, while the Pennsylvania system, under the guidance of that master hand, Alexander J. Cassatt, worked in complete harmony with all the other large railroad interests.

The intercorporate relationships of the railways

reached their highest point before the panic of 1907. By the end of 1906, we find that of a total railroad stock capitalization of about twelve billions of dollars, more than one-third was owned by the railroads themselves. In the cases of competing or parallel systems, minority interests of sufficient amount were held to create a substantial if not a dominating interest; but in the case of non-competing lines, or connecting lines, majority control was often effected. The latter was the case in New England, where the New York, New Haven and Hartford system, under Morgan influence, had acquired complete control of practically all the means of transportation, including the many coastwise steamship lines.

This remarkable welding together of great corporate interests could not, of course, have been accomplished if the "masters of capital" in Wall Street had not themselves during the same period become more closely allied. The rivalry of interests which was so characteristic during the reorganization period a few years before had very largely disappeared. Although the two great groups of financiers, represented on the one hand by Morgan and his allies and on the other by the Standard Oil forces, were still distinguishable, they were now working in practical harmony on the basis of a sort of mutual "community of interest" of their own. Thus the control of capital and credit through banking resources tended to become concentrated in the hands of fewer and fewer men.

The machinery for the control of credit had become steadily more effective since the days of the Steel Trust merger. Two groups of banks, partially allied but still independent, had been reaching out through the entire country. The National City Bank, now under the management of Frank A. Vanderlip, James Stillman having practically retired, had grown tremendously in power and with unusual rapidity. It had formed connections with large institutions in various cities of the country and had brought under its control several great trust companies. The growth of the Morgan banks and trust companies during this period was no less notable.

In the same period began a contest for the control of life insurance assets. In earlier days the life insurance business had occupied a modest place in the American financial world. The old, solid companies had grown steadily and quietly year by year, increasing their patronage and adding to their assets in a staid, conservative way. But they were generally looked upon as a thing apart, so far as banking connections or general financing were concerned. The old Equitable Life Assurance Society, although near the Wall Street district, was as distinct from Wall Street influences as though it had been located in Hartford or in Philadelphia; and the same was practically true of the Mutual Life Insurance Company and the New York Life Insurance Company. The investments of these large and growing companies, as well as those of a myriad of smaller ones, had from time out of mind been confined to government and municipal bonds and the highest grade of railroad securities. Each year had seen the surpluses of these companies grow, but as a matter of course their large cash resources were looked upon as unavailable for ordinary financial purposes. While the laws regulating the investment of life insurance funds were far more liberal than those pertaining to the investment of savings bank funds, yet Wall Street did not regard the one as any more liquid or available than the other for its own uses. As late as 1889 it appears that very little attention had been paid to the possibility of making use, in financial schemes, of the large liquid assets of these great companies.

But in the early nineties the trust company movement began to get vigorously under way.   Trust
companies, formed as they were under unusually
liberal banking laws, could not only compete with
the ordinary state banks and the national banks
in doing a straight banking business — receiving
deposits, discounting notes, and making loans on
collateral — but were fully empowered to do many
other lucrative things.   They were perfectly free,
for example, to "underwrite" financial schemes
and to take large interests in promotions or financial enterprises of a more or less speculative nature.
Such underwritings or promotions frequently yield-
ed fabulous profits, and it was quickly seen that the
stock of a modern trust company was likely to pay
larger dividends than that of a bank, which operated
under rigidly restrictive laws.

These possibilities for lucrative profits began
to be more fully demonstrated as the readjust-
ment and reorganization period set in about 1893.
Up to that time trust companies had made a special
feature of acting as fiscal and financial agents,
paying coupons, dividends, and performing the
general work of trusteeship for both corporate
and individual interests.   But now they began to
be the headquarters for bondholders' committees

and the agencies for reorganization committees and the like. Soon a further step was taken; abandoning the mere rôle of trustee, they began to be reorganizers and financiers of corporations directly. Profits flowed in, the stocks of the trust companies began to soar, and trust company dividends ranged far higher than did old-line bank dividends. An investment in the stock of a large Wall Street trust company became far more lucrative than an investment in a first class bank of the old style. So trust companies began to be formed with great rapidity.

But to form large companies with great resources and substantial reserves required much money. They were a new thing, and the type of individual investor who was perfectly willing to put money into a national or state bank was inclined to hesitate before embarking on this new enterprise. But money must be got somewhere; so the shrewd minds identified with or attracted by the possibilities of the movement began to search for untouched resources of some kind. Some success was achieved in getting Standard Oil money into the field, but only to a limited extent. For a while it looked as though the trust company business would have to take the usual course of any new business with money-making ideas and prove its stability with the lapse of time before it could hope to take a permanent place in American financial affairs.

Suddenly a new and unexpected source of capital opened. Identified with certain of the large life insurance companies of New York, either as presidents or managers, were a number of men of the purely financial type, men who were more or less involved in Wall Street interests and enterprises. These men, with their swelling insurance assets, were constantly looking for investments for the surplus funds of their companies; and they were not, as a rule, averse to making private fortunes for themselves. Though the life insurance laws restricted them to some extent in the use of the policyholders' money, so that they could not, as a private banker might, make use of this money in any really free and speculative way, it was perfectly legitimate for a life insurance company to invest its funds in any company operating under the banking laws. There was therefore nothing to prevent the Mutual Life or the Equitable Life from holding the stock of a trust company. And as the value of the capital stock of a bank or trust company in those days depended largely upon the character of its management or the personnel of its board of directors, it was soon found that a trust company which was openly identified with a large and powerful insurance concern would be assured of success.

Life insurance money thus began to go into trust companies, and officers and directors of life insurance companies began to take conspicuous places as directors of trust companies. And in addition, these new directors began to grow rich; and they grew rich in many cases where at the start they had no capital whatever. In forming a new trust company or in enlarging an old one by the issue of new stock, they not only would have their insurance company subscribe to a majority of the stock but would themselves subscribe to a minority on the same terms, and then deposit their own stock as collateral for a loan which they would obtain from their own insurance company. It would not in all cases be necessary for them to deposit any cash "margin" in the loan, for almost invariably the stock would be sold to them, as to the insurance company, at a figure considerably below its market value.

At that time there were no restrictive laws which forbade an officer of a corporation to borrow money from his own company on collateral, and the president or director of an insurance company was perfectly free to make use of the funds of his own company provided he deposited necessary security. And as he was himself the authority who scrutinized the collateral, it will be seen that his path was generally a very easy one.

During the period from about 1890 to the opening of the new century, this flow of life insurance money into the coffers of the trust companies increased rapidly. And as time went on, the movement took on new phases. The life insurance company, with its enormous cash assets, naturally favored its own trust companies in the matter of bank deposits and banking business generally. And as the trust companies had also begun to go largely into the investment business and dealt in stocks and bonds with practically the same freedom that a private investment banker did, it was not long before practically all the investing of life insurance funds was being done through the subsidiary trust companies. Naturally, in many cases the chief desire of the directors and large individual stockholders of the trust companies (who were also directors or officers of the parent life insurance companies) was to make big profits for the trust companies; so that, in many cases, the insurance companies were discriminated against in the matter of prices by their own directors or trustees.

But discrimination did not stop here. As we have seen, the trust companies early became promoters, financial underwriters, and controllers of big schemes. This sort of work involved the use of much capital; and the tendency was to get more and more life insurance money into the coffers of the trust companies, so that the latter would have plenty of funds to work with. There was "big money" in these things for the trust companies, but the life insurance companies often received only the normal rate of interest on their fat deposits which were used to make unheard-of profits for their own directors.

Notwithstanding the fact that trust companies and interlocking directors were growing rich through this use of insurance funds, the life insurance companies also continued to prosper. It was a period when practically the whole country was prospering, when New York City especially was waxing richer and richer, and when more and more men were not only taking out policies but were going into the life insurance business. Extraordinary efforts were continuously made by the great insurance companies to add to their lists of policyholders and to increase their surpluses. Naturally, all life insurance directorates which were also interested in trust companies and in Wall Street affairs generally, wanted to see the funds of their companies flow in a never ceasing stream, and they developed the most efficient and far-reaching organizations for getting new business.

By 1900 the assets of the great life insurance companies in New York City had begun to loom large in Wall Street operations. At the beginning of the movement we have been following, many more or less inconspicuous men were identified with it, but it was not long before the larger banking powers of Wall Street began to realize the possibilities in the control of life insurance assets. Prior to 1890 the "big three" New York companies — the Mutual, the Equitable, and the New York Life — had few conspicuous banking affiliations. But about that time, the Morgan house began to identify itself more closely with the New York Life, whose new president, John A. McCall, became known before very long as a Morgan man. The Equitable Life had had its various banking affiliations, and its president, Henry B. Hyde, was fairly close to Wall Street affairs. It had early become the controlling factor in the Mercantile

Trust Company, which, prior to the reorganization period, had been prominent chiefly as a conservative, "old-line" trust company, confining itself almost exclusively to the original business of performing the work of trustee and agent, to which its banking and deposit business was only incidental. The Mutual Life, with Richard A. McCurdy at its head, had grown steadily and solidly, but it was not until the early nineties that its name became identified with a trust company or Wall Street business. About this time, however, a small trust company, known as the New York Guarantee and Indemnity Company, came under the control of the Mutual Life. Its title was changed to that of the Guaranty Trust Company, and certain trustees of the Mutual Life Insurance Company became prominent in its directorate. Its capital was enlarged, and with the new connection its credit improved and its business grew by leaps and bounds. The control of the United States Mortgage and Trust Company was also acquired by the Mutual Life and its business also took a spurt.

In the course of time, many trust companies of less prominence became identified with the insurance companies, and finally, Wall Street bankers and financiers of the influential type began to flood the directorates of the insurance companies and the trust companies alike. Then came the period of big financing, the decade of consolidation and merger, followed by several years of feverish speculative activity in Wall Street and vast schemes of promotion. All the large bankers were soon on the finance committees of the life insurance companies — such men as J. P. Morgan, several of his partners, Jacob H. Schiff of Messrs. Kuhn, Loeb and Co., Henry C. Frick, Edward H. Harriman, and the Rockefeller representatives — indeed, all the big captains and masters of Wall Street.

Life insurance assets had now become a large factor in high finance and a vital part of the movement toward the control and capitalization of industry in general. Banking power, as identified with the different groups, now implied the control not merely of groups of national banks and trust companies but also of the life insurance companies with large assets and growing resources. Not only were the "big three" involved in this steadily growing concentration of power, but other large companies, such as the Metropolitan Life, the Prudential Life of Newark, and several companies in more distant cities, were becoming assets of importance to the big contending groups in Wall Street.

During that remarkable period from 1898 to 1904, when the industrial and commercial enterprises were being more and more heavily capitalized, when fabulous individual fortunes were being piled up, and when concentration of the control of finance was rapidly hastening to its climax, the assets of the insurance companies were handled with steadily increasing recklessness. At first considerable caution had been shown in the use of these large sums, but towards the end of the period they were more freely used in speculative and uncertain enterprises. Both money and credit were getting scarce under the strain of continued capitalization and promotion; and in Wall Street the period of "undigested" and "indigestible" securities was arriving. Private bankers were not so eager to secure large allotments in underwriting syndicates; large bond and stock issues did not go so well with the public as formerly. And yet all the giant promoters, the Harrimans, the Morgans, and their allies, needed cash and credit to carry through vast enterprises. Naturally, therefore, insurance assets, on which there was little or no restriction, were used more and more. Not only were insurance companies of great strength "allotted" abnormally large amounts of syndicate underwritings and securities by their own trustee bankers, but their subsidiary trust companies and other financial dependencies were also loaded up in the same way. The method became so free and easy that a great banking house engaged in carrying through some gigantic operation would simply "allot" to a certain insurance company a specified amount of bonds or other securities and would then instruct its president or trustees to take them, willy-nilly.

Naturally, this loose and extravagant method of making use of hundreds of millions of dollars belonging to hundreds of thousands of policyholders bred extravagance and corruption in the ranks of the smaller minds in the insurance organizations. In the great companies particularly, extravagance, waste, and inefficiency steadily grew. Millions of dollars were spent annually in elaborate furnishings for executive offices; all sorts of useless positions were created for retainers and worthless officers and clerks; money was wasted in buildings, in useless advertising, and in many other ways. Graft in a thousand forms began to creep in.

In 1903 occurred a semi-panic in the Wall Street security markets. Business had fallen off noticeably in the industrial world; the railroads staggered

in many cases under the heavy capitalizations
created during the speculative period of the few
years previous; and money was scarce and high.
President Roosevelt had attacked the Northern
Securities merger, and the Government had started
suit for its dissolution.   The great Steel Trust had
fallen on evil days, and its stocks and bonds had
dropped helter-skelter to low levels.   This was a
period of "undigested securities," and pessimism
reigned everywhere.

Because of the scarcity of capital and the low
credit of many concerns, a feeling of unrest and in-
security prevailed in financial circles.   Some outside interests began to investigate the stability of
large concerns; and some banking and trust company
failures ensued.   Then the security holdings of insurance companies, which were obliged to file annual reports and lists of their securities, began to
be closely scrutinized, and it was realized that the
large companies were loaded up with many unprofitable syndicate accounts and large investments which had undergone vast depreciation.
Criticism soon became rampant, and various suits
were started against companies and officials.   But
little change occurred until the following year,
when strenuous efforts began to be made for a

thorough investigation of the affairs and methods of the companies.

A sensational insurance investigation which began in 1905 lasted for several months. Under the direction of Charles E. Hughes, it disclosed to the public the entire inside history of life insurance finance during the previous decade, with all its high finance, reckless manipulation of funds, waste, extravagance, and graft. The result of this investigation was that new and far more stringent laws were enacted looking to the safeguarding of the assets of policyholders and the proper investment of insurance funds.

Thus, at one stroke, a prolific source of free and unrestricted cash was cut off from the speculator and promoter. The hundreds of millions which had for years been bandied about at the beck and call and to the profit of small groups of powerful men were no longer available.

The investigation of the insurance companies, with its results, was undeniably one of the factors which helped to save the situation when the panic of 1907 arrived. Had not the reckless financial methods of handling insurance funds been curbed a few years before, the crash of 1907 would have been far more disastrous than it proved.

The insurance companies were still loaded with large amounts of unsalable securities, but they bought no more, and under strict legal restrictions in the course of time they liquidated most of their dangerous assets without material loss.

CHAPTER VIII

IT is not to be assumed that the concentration of banking power and the control of corporate activities had no unfortunate accompaniments. Unquestionably the consolidation of the great railroad systems of the country, under the "community of interest" plan, resulted in greatly stabilizing freight rates; it increased efficiency of operation; it enabled the managements to develop large amounts of new business and to show greatly increased profits; and it bred a spirit of invincible optimism in Wall Street. The large crops of these years, the unusually heavy tide of foreign immigration, and the boom in business generally, all helped to increase this feeling of optimism in Wall Street. Great material progress and prosperity, however, inevitably invite speculation; and speculation, once begun, grows by what it feeds on.

In the closing months of 1904 a great speculative

movement in the stock market began and continued
almost without interruption through 1905 and well
into 1906. The prices of railroad stocks soared
to unheard-of heights; Great Northern preferred
rose above 300; Northern Pacific above 200; St.
Paul to nearly 200; Atchison, Southern Pacific,
Union Pacific, New York Central, and the rest all
steadily climbed to higher and higher levels. Industrial stocks, also, were having their day, and
new enterprises were being floated in Wall Street
by the hundred. Credit was easy to obtain; interest rates were low; and after 1905, most of the
bankers and speculative investors had become so
accustomed to high prices and large speculative
profits that almost any financial "proposition"
found ready acceptance in Wall Street.

It was a new day for the underwriting syndicate,
and brokers eagerly sought for opportunities to underwrite anything that promised profits, regardless of its merit. Many undertakings of extremely
doubtful or speculative nature were passed along
as sound without any real investigation whatever.
Many private banking firms, even of relatively conservative reputation, acquired the habit of join-
ing in questionable underwritings. The new era of
banking control, moreover, had brought with it a

superficial notion that financial panics like those of 1873 and 1893 could never again occur. It was frequently said that the coördination of American industry, under the control of powerful banking institutions, would always be a safeguard against the dangers of inflation and over-speculation. Yet in 1906 financial America was in a very true sense riding for a fall.

The United States Shipbuilding Company, known as "the Shipbuilding Trust," illustrates the speculative spirit which was undermining the financial credit of the country. This was a combination of shipbuilding manufacturers, promoted on the theory that Congress, under the control of the Republican party, would soon pass a liberal ship-subsidy law which would be followed by a great revival in shipbuilding. This expectation had also buoyed up Morgan's International Mercantile Marine Company formed in 1902. No legislation of the sort took place; but the promoters of "the Shipbuilding Trust" continued their efforts with undiminished fervor. A young man named Daniel Le Roy Dresser organized the Trust Company of the Republic and attempted to underwrite this United States Shipbuilding Company. Eight companies, one or two of which were fairly valuable, the rest being largely heaps of junk, were merged in the combination, the capitalization of which was colossal. An enormous bonded debt was created to raise funds to buy up the operating companies at high valuations. One small plant, which the owners a year before would have been glad to sell for $100,000, was bought up at a valuation of over $2,000,000, one-quarter of which was paid in cash.

The United States Shipbuilding Company had hardly been formed when it began to fall to pieces. The underwriters were not able to make good. Then to the astonishment of everybody, its president, Lewis Nixon, announced that the company had bought the Bethlehem Steel Company from Charles M. Schwab. This seemed incredible, as the Bethlehem Steel Company was of more tangible value than the whole outfit of shipbuilding plants. Everybody thought Schwab was crazy, for he was to be paid, so it was generally understood, in bonds of the United States Shipbuilding Company, which promised to be worthless. But Schwab was far from crazy. He had insisted that the bonds carry voting power. Presently, when the whole scheme went down with a crash, carrying with it the Trust Company of the Republic,

Schwab was found in possession of the entire group of plants, including the Bethlehem Steel. He then lopped off the worthless properties and attached the good shipbuilding plants as subsidiaries to the Bethlehem Steel Company.

Another and equally unsound type of promotion was going on in banking. A number of smaller financiers, trying to copy Morgan and Standard Oil, would form a chain of banks with unlimited capital, to promote their speculations. Notable among these speculative bankers was Charles W. Morse, a man of unusual ability. He had made a large fortune in the American Ice Company and in the manipulation of its securities in Wall Street; he had also done something in shipbuilding and operating steamships. By 1905 he had reached a position of substantial power in Wall Street. He acquired control of the Bank of North America, one of Wall Street's old and solid institutions, and began to make use of this bank's credit and resources for financing his promotions. Finding himself in need of more capital, he acquired control of other banks by making use of the resources of the banks he already owned or controlled. By the close of 1906, he had under his own sway, or that of his close friends, seven or eight good banks, besides having considerable influence in a number of others. He then launched an ambitious scheme for consolidating all the coastwise steamship lines on the Atlantic seaboard, paying fabulously high prices for these lines and capitalizing them to the moon. Having thus acquired nearly everything afloat from Maine to Florida, he bought from Morgan all the stock of the Central of Georgia Railroad Company in order to get control of the Ocean Steamship Company, a line which operated from Savannah to New York and connected with the Central of Georgia.

Meanwhile the great pot in Wall Street went boiling on. In the summer of 1906 the Harriman financiers added fuel to the fire by suddenly increasing from six to ten per cent the dividend on Union Pacific common, thus sending that stock up forty points practically overnight. Discretion in Wall Street was thrown to the winds; many of the most conservative houses began to push securities of more and more doubtful types. A mining stock craze broke out, and in a few months the whole country was madly buying up worthless shares in a thousand or more gold and silver mines at ridiculously high prices and without thought of investigation. The Wall Street "curb" became a bedlam of mining brokers, and even the Stock Exchange gave dignity to a number of mining ventures by listing their stocks. [1]

Long before the close of 1906 there were ominous signs of danger ahead, and many thoughtful men began to urge caution. The wild speculation caused a steadily increasing strain on credit, and demand loans in Wall Street rose in September to the highest figure they had reached in years. In the same month, the New York banks reported a deficit in reserves and appealed to the United States Treasury for surplus gold. This timely deposit afforded temporary relief; but the year closed in strain. Most of the Wall Street bankers, however, persisted in the theory that fundamentally everything was sound, that the outlook for 1907 was distinctly hopeful, and that after the turn of the New Year all would be well.

Wall Street financiers, high and low, seemed to be hypnotized by the long period of easy money, rising prices, quickly made fortunes, and successful

[1] The immediate cause of the mining stock boom was the discovery, in the previous year, of the great silver deposits in the Cobalt region of Canada and the gold deposits in the Goldfield region of Nevada. A few companies, such as the Nipissing mines in Canada and the Jumbo mine in Nevada, were real bonanzas and paid millions in time to their stockholders, but nearly all the others sooner or later turned out to be worthless.

promotions. Harriman certainly did not foresee any bad turn in affairs, for in 1906 he caused the Union Pacific and Southern Pacific companies to employ their large surpluses in buying large additional blocks of railroad stocks at top prices; the Morgan and Hill interests did not seem to foresee trouble, for they were developing their railroad properties and spending money like water on improvements; the City Bank or Standard Oil masters did not gauge the future accurately, for they were not only doing nothing to stem the tide of speculation, but were actually floating various schemes of their own on the current. Certainly smaller and more speculative men, like Charles W. Morse, Charles M. Schwab, F. Augustus Heintze, and Charles T. Barney of the Knickerbocker Trust Company did not fear the future, for they were extending their operations in all directions. Schwab had gone into mining on a large scale; Heintze was promoting a balloon known as the United Copper Company, aided by the credit of the Mercantile National Bank, control of which he had acquired; Morse was floating his ship bubble; and Barney was sinking the funds of the great Knickerbocker Trust Company in all sorts of unsound ventures.

Little change in conditions occurred until February, 1907, but with the opening of the month the stock market began to crumble, and the banks commenced to call in loans and mend their fences. But the real unsoundness of the day was not understood until, a few weeks later, Henry H. Rogers, vice-president of the Standard Oil Company, found difficulty in securing a loan of twenty million dollars for his Virginian railway, which he was at that time building to open up some soft-coal fields in the western part of the State. Rogers had to pay an equivalent of over eight per cent for this loan, secure it with over thirty million dollars of the highest grade investment stocks and bonds, and personally endorse the notes, though his credit was as high as that of any man in the United States. This transaction created consternation. If the vice-president of the Standard Oil Company, that great reservoir of ready cash, had to go into the market for a pittance like twenty million dollars and pay over eight per cent for it, then indeed things were in bad shape.

The "March panic," or "silent panic" as it was called, immediately followed. Stocks dropped three to ten points at a time; money rates reached a great height; banks closed their doors to borrowers;

and stockbrokers began to fail. Speculators by the thousands were wiped out; the mining boom on the "curb" completely collapsed; and in Wall Street financiers were seen daily and hourly, rushing hither and thither, trying to devise ways and means to weather the storm. But the high money rates drew gold from Europe; the Secretary of the Treasury deposited further funds in New York banks; and as the crop-moving period had ended, funds naturally gravitated to New York City, and thus helped to relieve the situation. The panic was stayed for the time being.

Wall Street still refused to believe that any further trouble was ahead. Business throughout the country continued at high pressure; railroad earnings were large, and industries were booming; the new crop outlook was favorable; and while money rates were high, there seemed to be enough at the moment to go round. Even the big "masters of capital," although following a more cautious policy, seemed to think that the worst was over. Nearly everybody said, "Wall Street has now cleaned house; we will soon be in a bigger boom than ever." All seemed to base their reasoning on the idea that, with industry and business going on prosperously, any further trouble in Wall Street was unthinkable.

After the 1st of July, however, there were developments which created disquietude in high places. The United States Steel Corporation reported an alarming falling off in unfilled tonnage; railroad earnings suddenly began to sag; then the money market tightened up, and the fear became widespread that the fast approaching crop-moving period would create a great money stringency. Presently came the collapse of Charles W. Morse's shipping combination. Then, to cap the climax, came the failure of the City of New York to sell a large block of bonds in Wall Street. Altogether August was an uneasy month for the "masters of capital" and for their thousands of satellites and followers.

September saw the heads of big business often in consultation; the powers were at last awake to the seriousness of the situation. The newspapers were urged to talk encouragingly; Wall Street interviews were uniformly optimistic. Clearly, strenuous efforts were being made to tide over the crisis. But to no avail. In October came the Heintze failure, involving first the Mercantile National Bank and then the whole Heintze-Morse chain of banks. Next occurred the run on the Knickerbocker Trust Company, the suicide of its president, and the closing of its doors. Then followed in quick succession the failure of the National Bank of North America and runs on the Trust Company of America, the Lincoln Trust Company, and a dozen other institutions. All these disasters involved banks in other cities and pulled down private firms and brokers. The accompanying panic in the stock market completed the havoc. The holocaust was on.

The small group of mighty financiers — the men who had been chiefly responsible for the building up of the great concentrated system of banking power, corporate control, community of interests, and interlocking relationships, all of which had finally culminated in this terrific smash — these were the men whose powers were now to be taxed to save financial America. The morning after the Knickerbocker smash, while the run on the Trust Company of America was filling all Wall Street with crowds of excited depositors, a man walked into the office of J. P. Morgan and Company, pushed past the guard, and entered Morgan's private room. Morgan nodded and said, "Good morning, Mr. Frick." The two men talked quietly for perhaps ten minutes. Frick went away; then Edward H. Harriman came in. Following him came other "masters," one by one or in pairs. Finally came James Still-man, president of the National City Bank and spokesman for the great Standard Oil interests.

That day many millions of dollars were doled out to the banks by the Secretary of the Treasury; government bonds were supplied by institutions and private investors for temporary use, John D. Rockefeller alone lending ten million dollars' worth. Then both Morgan and Stillman made arrangements to buy bills of exchange in enormous quantities, and force gold shipments from Europe. These measures began the relief which the situation needed.

Yet one of the gravest dangers remained. This was the position of the brokerage firm of Moore and Schley, involved in a big speculative pool in the stock of the Tennessee Coal, Iron and Railroad Company. Moore and Schley had pledged over six millions of the Tennessee Coal and Iron stock for loans among the Wall Street banks. The banks had called the loans, and the firm could not pay, as was of course known to Morgan and the others. If Moore and Schley should fail, a hundred more failures would follow and then all Wall Street might go to pieces. The only thing to do was to save Moore and Schley.

The Tennessee Coal, Iron and Railroad Company was one of the chief competitors of United States Steel and it owned enormously valuable iron and coal deposits. It was Morgan's plan, in which Frick, Harriman, and the others agreed, to buy the Tennessee stock from Moore and Schley. In this way the panic could be stayed and a big stroke of good business done for the greater corporation. Gary was called in to discuss the matter. The only obstacle seemed to be the Government. Would a purchase of this kind be construed as a violation of the Sherman Act? A deputation, consisting of Gary, Perkins, and others, was dispatched to Washington to lay the matter before President Roosevelt. The President promised immunity and the purchase was then immediately consummated. The United States Steel Corporation paid thirty million dollars in its own bonds for the Tennessee stock; these bonds were accepted as collateral by the bank where the Tennessee stock had been refused; and the firm of Moore and Schley was saved. The announcement had an immediate effect, and from that hour matters began to mend.

Before the turn of the new year, Wall Street was normal again. The prices of securities had rallied substantially, the money market had grown much easier, fear and fright had disappeared, and men were looking forward with confidence into the future. And, as the year 1908 wore on, it became evident that the panic marked the culmination of "high finance." The great banking groups were still intact, to be sure, and their influence and power seemed as far-reaching as ever. But the glamour of speculation and promotion had largely disappeared. The shock of the panic had put conservatism into the survivors and of course a great horde of speculators had fallen.

Yet there was still rivalry between Harriman and Morgan. In the fall of 1908 Harriman induced the Mutual Life Insurance Company to sell him half of the working control of the great Guaranty Trust Company, with its one hundred million of assets. And in the early part of the following year Harriman obtained an option on a half interest in the control of the Equitable Life Assurance Society. Harriman evidently proposed to form a banking power greater even than that of the National City Bank or of the Morgans, as a part of a colossal scheme which he was developing. The control of the Union Pacific system, the greatest railroad system on the American continent — for the Union Pacific at that time controlled two lines to the Atlantic seaboard — did not satisfy this man's ambition. He was working for a world railroad empire. Before the panic year Harriman had made his control of the Baltimore and Ohio practically secure. During the dark days of the panic he had taken over from Charles W. Morse the stock of the Central of Georgia and had made this railroad a subsidiary of the Illinois Central. Now he was planning a railroad system in Asia which would connect with the Siberian Railway in Russia and finally work through to the capitals of Europe. He had already secured an option on the South Manchurian Railway in China and was endeavoring to obtain the coöperation and backing of the Japanese Government to further his plans.

Had Harriman lived, no one knows what might have occurred in railroad history during the following few years. But he was playing a very difficult game and the strain was beginning to tell on him. In the summer of 1909 he was taken seriously ill and died in the early fall. The death of Harriman caused an almost immediate change in the banking situation in New York. Within three months Morgan and his associates had bought Harriman's stock in the Guaranty Trust Company and with it the holdings of the Mutual Life Insurance Company.

Later Morgan acquired from Thomas F. Ryan control of the Equitable Life Assurance Society, which had fallen into Ryan's hands in 1905. Thus we find Morgan in practical control of the "Big Three" in life insurance in New York, for he had already dominated the New York Life for many years. He then merged the Morton and the Fifth Avenue Trust companies into the Guaranty and this union gave him and his associates a dominating position among the trust companies of New York, since he already controlled the powerful and growing Bankers Trust Company, which had been formed a few years before. These moves also resulted in giving him a closer grip on the affairs of the National Bank of Commerce.

This growth of the Morgan banking power did not, however, excite any spirit of competition or rivalry between his interests and those of Standard Oil, for the time had passed when rivalry in banking was the fashion. Before long it could be said, indeed, that two rival banking groups no longer existed, but that one vast and harmonious banking power had taken their place.

Harriman was now dead; Henry H. Rogers was dead; Alexander J. Cassatt, the great Pennsylvania Railroad president, was dead; James Stillman

had retired from active business; William Rockefeller was no longer an active business promoter.
Times were changing and new men were coming to
the front. Frank A. Vanderlip, the young head of
the National City Bank, was becoming more and
more the spokesman for the Rockefeller interests;
George W. Perkins was still active with the Morgans, but the strong personality of Henry P. Davison was beginning to dominate the firm. Though
Morgan himself remained in command until his
death in 1913, he was clearly growing old and
was placing more and more responsibility on his
younger partners.

These newer men in Wall Street were not the
products of the old time, when experience was
gained by building up and welding together the
parts of the vast modern industrial and banking
machine. They had not been educated in the hard
and struggling school for mastery through which
Morgan and Frick and Harriman and Rockefeller
had come. When they arrived, they found the financial machine already in motion; their work was to
perfect it and keep it well oiled. Consequently,
with the arrival of the new and younger school of
financiers, a less spectacular season set in for Wall
Street. Money power increased; intercorporate

relationships were maintained; but few further steps were taken in elaborating or developing the system.

Long before the panic of 1907, political rumblings had reached the ears of Wall Street. In President Roosevelt's first term, the Sherman Act had been invoked against the Northern Securities Company, and that gigantic product of the spirit of consolidation had been dissolved by decree of court. A little later, new powers were given to the Interstate Commerce Commission over the operation of the railroads, and for the first time the Commission was fully empowered to regulate freight rates. The New York insurance investigation under Charles E. Hughes, with its astonishing disclosures, had shown growing public aversion to the methods of "high finance."

The panic, with its accompanying disasters, had a large share in prompting the Government at Washington to take action against the trusts; and before Roosevelt left the White House in 1909 suits had been brought against a large number of industrial trusts, including Standard Oil and Tobacco. Later, suits were instituted against the Steel Trust, the Harvester Trust, and a great many others. When Taft became President in 1909, many of the big combinations formed during the previous decade were practically under indictment. In 1911 the Supreme Court ordered the dissolution of Standard Oil and Tobacco and of a large number of smaller trusts as well. These decisions brought about radical changes in the character of the corporations. The original subsidiary companies were obliged to take over the properties under nominally competitive conditions. Such dissolutions proved in the end, however, to be mere changes of form, for the various companies involved continued to be owned, controlled, and managed by practically the same men, with little if any real competition.

Later a drive against the railroads began in the same way; the Union Pacific was forced to disgorge its interest in the Southern Pacific Company, and the Pennsylvania disposed of its control in its competitor, the Baltimore and Ohio. The new federal laws regulating freight rates made the "community of interest" plan of interlocking control of little use, so that the different railroads began liquidating their interest in other properties to a large extent. Within a few years, the ties binding together the big trunk lines and larger systems were steadily loosened. And finally, Federal statutes prohibiting interlocking directorates, not only among competing railroad systems, but among banks and industrial concerns, completed the process of "unscrambling the eggs." Before the World War opened, the long chapter of "high finance," as understood during the wild and dramatic days of 1901 to 1906, had practically closed.

CHAPTER IX

WAR is the great revealer; it demonstrates, as does nothing else, the strength and weakness of a nation, material and spiritual. The first two years of the First World War clearly disclosed the financial and industrial greatness of the United States; the last two years happily showed that the nation was great in other things than money, munitions, and food. Yet it became apparent, even in the days of American neutrality, that the support of American agriculture and industry was practically indispensable to the allied cause. America possessed the largest available supply of that copper, steel, cotton, and food without which the armies of the Entente would have struggled in vain. Wall Street became, at least temporarily, the international money market; more than a third of all the gold in the world soon found its way to New York; and the United States which, since the Revolution, had

been a debtor nation, soon discovered that Europe
owed her far more money than she had ever owed
Europe. The mere fact that, in 1916, the United
States produced 43,000,000 tons of steel, while
Great Britain, which normally ranks next to this
country in steel manufacture, produced 9,000,000
tons, not only indicates the extent to which American industry had expanded under the pressure of
war, but gives some indication of the part which it
was playing on European battlefields. Thus, long
before American armies gave Marshal Foch that
superiority in men which turned the balance from
defeat to victory, American mines, American steel
mills, American farms, and American money had
become powerful elements in the war.

Wall Street awoke rather slowly to its new position as a maker of history. Its first reaction to
the European nightmare was one of bewilderment
and panic. In this it merely reflected the mental
state of the European bourses of which it had been
a dependent for many years. The hardest headed
American business man had difficulty in keeping
his poise when all the Stock Exchanges of Europe
had closed their doors and when the news ticker
reported a run upon the Bank of England. Wall
Street had never faced such a crisis as that which

dawned on the morning of August 3, 1914. Only once in its history of more than a hundred years had this great market suspended operations, and then only for a few days during the panic of 1873. But the conditions facing it in August, 1914, were unparalleled. The Kaiser's ultimatums to Russia and France, making war inevitable, caused European investors to rush their securities to the London stock market, which averted a panic only by closing. Since all the important markets of Europe and South America followed the London example, there remained only one place in the world where stocks could be sold — New York. At that time European investors, for the larger part British, held at least $4,000,000,000 of American securities. There was not the slightest question that they would attempt to dispose of these on almost any terms. There are experts now who believe that the American market could then have stood this strain, but there were few who entertained such encouraging ideas in August, 1914. The prevailing opinion then was that all American securities would suffer such declines that a general calling of bank loans would result and that the country would be visited with the greatest financial and industrial panic in its history. Yet Wall

Street was kept in suspense for twenty-four hours. On Monday morning, the 3d of August, the usual aggregation of brokers, most of them in a high state of excitement, gathered on the floor. The gong which announces the beginning of business rings promptly at ten o'clock: the employee whose business it is to ring it stood stolidly at his post, having received no instructions not to give the signal. As the pointer on the clock passed fifteen minutes to ten and started towards the fatal hour, the nervous tension increased. The excited members all had vast quantities of stocks which they had been ordered to sell, and they trembled at what would happen when they threw these on the market. It was not until five minutes to ten that an officer of the Exchange stepped upon the floor and read the official notice that the market would be closed indefinitely. The cheer that went up eloquently voiced the relief which this step brought to a chaotic situation.

This closing indicated that the United States was still the financial dependent of Europe. The Exchange remained closed four months; then, on the 28th of November, it timidly opened its doors and began trading again in restricted fashion. Externally the position of Wall Street in November seemed to have changed little from its position in August. The great European exchanges were still closed; thus New York became the one market on which European holdings could be "dumped." Europe still held vast quantities of American securities on which it might be expected to realize. Yet, when the American market opened, something quite extraordinary took place. Europe, as was expected, began to sell American securities in large amounts, but stocks on Wall Street did not decline; instead, they advanced. The reopening of the Stock Exchange really started one of the most sensational stock "booms" in the history of that institution. Instead of having a panic on its hands, as many had freely predicted, Wall Street discovered that it had a bull market of unprecedented buoyancy. The real fact was that, in the intervening four months, the financial prestige of the United States had been enormously enhanced. Alone of all the great markets of the world Wall Street had not had to resort to the expedients that commonly accompany panic conditions. All European countries, including such a financial giant as Great Britain, had declared a moratorium, or a temporary suspension of the legal obligation to pay debts, and most South American

countries had resorted to the same expedient. No
moratorium had been declared in the United States.
Practically all European countries, even including
England, resorted to various currency expedients
that amounted practically to inflation. The United
States resorted to no such unscientific expedients
as it had tried in the Civil War but met the demands of the hour by supplying an elastic emergency currency under the terms of the new Federal
Reserve Act.[1] But certain developments even more
fundamental showed that this prosperity was not
fictitious. When war broke out, the United States
was harvesting the greatest wheat crop in its history, and at the same time the other great wheat
countries were showing a smaller production. The
closing of the Dardanelles kept Russia's wheat
from reaching its market. All the world now began
to bid for America's food supply, a demand immediately evidenced in the startling increase in our
export statistics. Meanwhile the allied nations began scouring the United States for all kinds of war
supplies. They found little in the way of guns or
ammunition, but they did find industrial plants

[1] Congress still further facilitated the issue of emergency currency
by amending the Federal Reserve Act. At the same time clear-
ing-house associations in the larger cities arranged for the issuing
of certificates.

far greater than those of any other country which could be very soon transformed into huge ammunition factories. War orders for all kinds of munitions started these plants going twenty-four hours a day, while orders for clothing and other indispensable materials of war put new life into such great industrial regions as New England. The result was a huge balance of trade in favor of the United States. The gold supply of Europe began to find its way into the coffers of Wall Street, a movement that was continuous until 1917, when, of the approximately $8,500,000,000 outstanding, nearly $3,000,000,000 was ultimately deposited in American safety vaults.

In the early days of the war England had practically abdicated, for the time being, the position of international banker which she had held for a hundred years. In a single year Lombard Street, up to the cataclysm of 1914, had invested over a billion dollars in new securities, domestic and foreign. Lombard Street had largely financed the building of American railroads, had contributed greatly to the financing of American enterprises of all kinds, had been a large purchaser of government and municipal bonds, not only in the United States, but in South American countries. That familiar annual phenomenon in the United States, known as "moving the crops," had been made possible for many years with credits supplied by England. But in the early part of 1915, the British Government vetoed all operations of this kind and informed the bankers that their resources must be used exclusively for war purposes. What market could thus step into the position of international banker which England by government fiat had surrendered? Two years before, any suggestion that Wall Street could do this would have been regarded as absurd; yet the American market adjusted itself to this position with comparative ease. It not only supplied home demands for ready money, but began making loans aggregating hundreds of millions to Canada, Switzerland, Norway, Sweden, and the South American republics. Wall Street bought the bond issues of Paris, Bordeaux, and Lyons, and even provided funds for international trade. Soon it had to meet new demands.

Up to 1914, Wall Street had played little part in financing foreign governments, its activities in this direction being limited almost to lending Great Britain $200,000,000 at the time of the South African War and Japan $50,000,000 at the time of the Russian War. But as the war orders of the Allies began flooding our markets, Great Britain and France attempted to pay for their purchases with cash, an expedient which drove British exchange up to a point which it had never reached in the history of the New York market. It soon became evident that, if the United States was to do business with the Allies on this huge scale, some other method must be adopted for settling the account. What this method should be was clear. Great Britain had built up her foreign trade largely by lending to her customers the money with which they purchased the goods. It was evident that we should have to do the same thing. The simplest way for the British and French Governments to establish credits in the United States with which to pay for war supplies would be to sell their bonds in our markets. The money obtained from sales, when deposited in American banks, could then be drawn upon for settlements. Simple as this device might seem in theory, it involved what seemed in 1915 to be insuperable difficulties. American investors had never shown any great eagerness to purchase government securities, excepting their own. There really existed no public market for such investments, in the sense that such a market had for so long existed in England, France, and other countries. Some of our supersensitive government officials at first believed that such an operation would be a violation of neutrality and a considerable pro-German element lifted up their voices in protest. There were others who questioned the soundness of the investment: the war threatened world-wide bankruptcy, and there was a fear that even so powerful a nation as Great Britain might not be able to pay her obligations. Nevertheless, in the latter part of 1915, a distinguished Anglo-French mission arrived in New York for the purpose of floating an American loan. The sum suggested, $1,000,000,000, staggered Wall Street; no Government had ever floated a foreign loan of such proportions. In accordance with the advice of American bankers the amount was cut to $500,000,-000, and this was disposed of successfully. From now on, all the purchases of the British and French were paid for in this way. After this credit was exhausted, these Governments continued to borrow in Wall Street, usually pledging American securities.

Not only did England and France pay for their supplies with money furnished by Wall Street, but they made their purchases through the same medium. As related in a previous chapter, the house of Morgan has always maintained close and confidential relations with the British Government and the British public. The necessity of buying materials by the billions in the United States soon produced a state of chaos in London. Contract hunters and contract jobbers pounced upon the British War Office; all kinds of irresponsible persons, American and European, obtained contracts for speculative purposes. Unless disaster was to result, it was evidently necessary to select some trustworthy agency in this country which could be depended upon to mobilize American industry, place the European orders in the right quarters, and attend to all the details. Inevitably the house of Morgan was selected for this important task. Thus the war had given Wall Street an entirely new rôle. Hitherto it has been exclusively the headquarters of finance; now it became the greatest industrial mart the world had ever known. In addition to selling stocks and bonds, financing railroads, and performing the other tasks of a great banking center, Wall Street began to deal in shells, cannon, submarines, blankets, clothing, shoes, canned meats, wheat, and the thousands of other articles needed for the prosecution of a great war. This new function brought to the front an American

business man who had hitherto been practically
unknown.   In looking for the man best qualified to conduct this purchasing campaign the
Morgan firm discovered Edward R. Stettinius,
the president of the Diamond Match Company.
Stettinius in turn searched American industry
for the men best qualified to assist him in his gigantic task, with the result that he got together a
force of 175, who organized themselves into a department known humorously as the "S.O.S." —
or "Slaves of Stettinius."   In a short time this
group found themselves purchasing supplies at the
rate of $10,000,000 a day.   To a considerable ex-
tent the materials in which this agency dealt had
never been made in the United States before, at
least in appreciable quantities.   They had to extend on a tremendous scale such munitions factories as already existed and to construct hundreds of entirely new plants.   American industry
adapted itself to the new demands speedily and
satisfactorily, and many concerns which had never
made munitions of any kind were soon turning
them out in perfect shape.   So successfully was the
work done that up to September, 1917, the Morgan firm had bought more than $3,000,000,000 in
merchandise and munitions and had, besides this,

marketed from $2,000,000,000 to $3,000,000,000 of American securities which had formerly been held by European investors.

With one American captain of industry the British Government dealt directly. He was a man whose name has already figured in this narrative. Indeed, next to J. Pierpont Morgan, the American business man who was best known in England was Charles M. Schwab. England understood even better than Americans the proportions of the Bethlehem Steel Company and the manufacturing genius of its head. When Kitchener became Minister of War, one of his first acts was to cable Schwab asking him to take the next boat for England. In a few days Schwab and Kitchener were closeted at the British War Office. The Secretary's demands were to the point. How many shells could Schwab supply? A million? Yes. How long would it take him? Ten months. Could Schwab furnish any guns? Yes, and quickly. In this way Kitchener rehearsed all his requirements and Schwab pledged all the capacity of the Bethlehem Steel plant. At the end of several days' conferences Kitchener approached a delicate point. He had only one anxiety about the Bethlehem Company, he said, and that was that German interests might purchase it.

Schwab immediately offered to sign an agreement that the Bethlehem Company would not be sold to any one so long as it had any British contracts under way. And so this American manufacturer with the German name became one of the strongest industrial allies of the British Government. According to the popular estimate he shipped not far from $300,-000,000 worth of war materials to England in less than two years. To do this he so increased his facilities that the Bethlehem Company presently became a larger munitions plant than the Krupps, and Schwab's shipyards alone had a capacity for turning out a larger tonnage than all the shipyards in Germany. One of his particularly interesting feats was the manufacture of twenty submarines, which were sent in parts to Canada, where they were pieced together and sent across the Atlantic under their own power. A year or so afterward Germany sent the submarine *Deutschland* to the United States and widely advertised the performance as something unprecedented!

Valuable as all this work was in promoting the cause of the Allies, it had one result that was still more important. For it prepared financial America for war. When Congress declared war on April 6, 1917, America, as a nation, had made little preparation for participating in the great conflict. We had an army only in skeleton; we had a navy efficient in its personnel and in its ships but entirely inadequate for the crisis; we had hardly any mercantile marine. In only one part of the United States had there been any real preparedness, and that was the part which had for decades been perhaps the most unpopular section of the country. From August, 1914, Wall Street had displayed an attitude that compares well with those elements in American life which had viciously assailed business and industry. With the exception of one or two German-backed banking houses, its sympathies had been enthusiastically with the Allies. And the part which it had played in financing the Allies laid the foundations for the work it did in the American period of participation. The outbreak in 1914 had produced the wildest chaos in European business and finance: stocks had tumbled, money rates had gone up, industry had ceased as though stricken with paralysis, and general dissolution had been prevented only, as we have seen, by resorting to a moratorium. But no such demoralization seized Wall Street when the United States declared war. Instead of falling, the stock market advanced — a movement generally hailed as a fair augury of victory. Never had America attained so sound and so preëminent a financial position. In two years we had ceased to be a debtor nation and now had Europe deeply in our debt. We had lent foreign Governments, bankers, and merchants not far from $2,000,000,000; yet so plentiful was money in New York that the investment bankers complained because they could not find enough securities to supply their customers. Of the $4,000,000,000 American securities estimated to have been held in England and France in 1914, we had purchased all but $1,000,000,000, and of this $300,000,000 had been pledged by the British and French Governments as securities for loans, while the remaining $700,000,000 lay in the government exchequers for similar use as occasion should arise. Thus there was no longer any danger that these stocks and bonds would be suddenly unloaded on the American market with disastrous results. At the beginning of the war our gold holdings amounted to $1,887,000,000, while by December 1, 1917, they had grown to $2,563,-000,000. Moreover, there was no likelihood that Europe could draw this away.

In recommending a declaration of war, President Wilson said that we should extend to the allied powers "the most liberal financial credits, in order that our own resources may so far as possible be added to theirs." At first it was thought that perhaps our chief help to the Allies would be financial and industrial. There were Germans, more enlightened than the Prussian militarists and diplomats, who did not regard such assistance with indifference. "We are mad," said Albert Ballin, the creator of the German mercantile marine, in 1917; "we have done a disastrous thing, a thing which will throw its shadow over our economic life for a generation. How are we to resume our foreign trade in the face of an Anglo-Saxondom which loathes and must loathe our presence among them? All the military victories and all the wild will-of-the-wisps about Hamburg to Bagdad will not help us."

"Almost uncanny" was the comment of a London observer on the quiet with which Wall Street accepted the declaration of war. But events had not progressed far when it became apparent that this attitude was justified.

The way in which America's entrance first tangibly affected the situation was that she immediately took over the burden which Great Britain had been carrying of financing the Allies. For

two and a half years Great Britain had not only
met her own expenditures, but had made advances
on a huge scale to France, Italy, Russia, Belgium,
Serbia, and the other Entente combatants.   The
United States not only assumed these responsibili-
ties, but began advancing enormous sums to Great
Britain herself.   These were not subsidies, such
as Pitt had given to England's allies in the Na-
poleonic wars; they were loans.   In reality, the
United States placed its credit at the disposal of
its fellow combatants.   It sold its own bonds in
the American market, advanced the money so obtained to the European powers, taking in exchange
their bonds at the same rate of interest.   The practical outcome of the operation was to save England, France, and the other borrowers great sums
in interest.   The several acts authorizing American
bond issues contained provisions empowering the
Treasury Department to make these loans to foreign governments; yet probably few imagined in
April, 1917, that these advances would ever be
so large.   The mere fact that the United States,
besides spending enormous sums on its own military preparations, was able to lend nearly $10,000,-
000,000 to European Governments in little less
than two years, gives some idea of the resources

which this country brought to bear in the European conflict. Despite these almost unimaginable expenditures, the nation, judging from all external signs, was suffering no discomforts, hardly any inconveniences, and there were no indications that the people could not withstand the strain indefinitely.

The fact was that financial America in 1919 was an entirely different nation from that of 1914. The successive bond issues had transformed us into a nation of investors. Despite the power which American finance had developed in the period of neutrality, there were many pessimists in 1917 who declared that the first popular Liberty Loan for $2,000,000,000 could never succeed. The American people, it was urged, were not thrifty; they had not developed the habit of purchasing government securities; floating bond issues in the United States had always been almost exclusively a banking undertaking. This statement was not quite historically correct. Indeed, the methods of popular subscription which had proved so successful in England were largely an American invention. The first man who used somewhat spectacular methods for selling government bonds to small holders was Jay Cooke, the great financier of the

Civil War. Cooke's most remarkable feat — perhaps the most remarkable of the kind until the outbreak of the European War — was his success in selling nearly $400,000,000 of the five-twenty bonds of 1863. In order to market this — as described in a preceding chapter — Cooke enlisted a force of from two thousand to three thousand canvassers, who visited all the towns and country districts of the United States and made personal solicitations from door to door, using handbills, posters, brass bands, and parades for advertising purposes. Energetic as Jay Cooke was, however, it required a persistent campaign of this kind finally to sell the issue; moreover, the bonds brought considerably less than par and the interest rate — six per cent — was high. This achievement had entirely passed out of the public mind by 1917, when the Secretary of the Treasury began raising $2,000,000,000 by similarly intensive methods. At first the gloomy prognostications of those who foretold failure seemed justified. Washington made the mistake of announcing that the public was rapidly oversubscribing the bonds, an announcement that naturally somewhat cooled popular enthusiasm. The financial houses of Wall Street, however, presently abandoned routine business and placed all their machinery behind the loan. In the last few days the subscriptions came in at a tremendous rate, the result being that the public which had been asked for $2,000,000,000 offered the Government over $3,000,000,000. The succeeding loans, for rapidly increasing amounts, were likewise phenomenally successful, the climax coming in November, 1918, on the eve of the armistice, when the American people, as the result of a three weeks' campaign, subscribed nearly $7,000,000,000 in a single issue. This is the largest loan ever recorded up to this time.

The united efforts of the whole American people, ranging all the way from the great Wall Street banking houses to vaudeville performers, made these loans successful. They indicated that Wall Street was no longer a circumscribed geographical district, but that — assuming that the phrase comprehends the financial resources of the United States — it included every town, every farm, every crossroads in the country. One of the most satisfactory by-products of the war, indeed, was the fact that it brought together many elements in our national life that had hitherto worked at cross purposes. It even diminished somewhat the widespread unpopularity of Wall Street. That the money power in the United States has many sins to answer for no rational person denies; happily for the forces of great wealth, the war gave them an opportunity to show that they, too, were American first of all and that they placed the prestige and dignity of their country above all personal sordid considerations. Only a few transparent demagogues and pro-Germans raised the cry that the struggle was "Wall Street's War." The Washington Administration at first showed some suspicion of the "interests," and for a time it attempted to reorganize its departments and prepare for the great struggle without the assistance of Big Business. This unfriendly disposition proved almost disastrous to the cause. It showed most conspicuously in the matter of building ships and airplanes — two things which seemed to be absolutely indispensable to success. Both these departments for a year were conducted by men who were entirely inadequate to the task. England had undergone a similar experience in the early days; she, too, when the war started, had found that all her big departments were headed by politicians, men who had little training in practical life and who were thus incompetent to transact that greatest of all modern enterprises — war. Gradually

Great Britain weeded out these men, replacing them for the most part by business leaders. Ultimately President Wilson adopted the same view. Strangely enough, one of the first appointees to go from Wall Street to an important Washington post belonged to precisely the class which had incurred the President's distrust. Bernard Baruch all his life had been primarily a Wall Street operator — a very successful one, it is true, but a man who had had absolutely no business training in the "constructive" sense. Even Wall Street itself gasped when it learned that the President had made Baruch the head of the War Industries Board, and, as such, the man who would do most of the purchasing in this country for the United States and the Allies. It is an evidence of the flexibility of the Wall Street temperament that Baruch, despite his lack of practical experience, made a success of his job. When the war ended, this official was buying war materials at the rate of $10,000,000,000 a year and was unquestionably the greatest "buyer" the world has ever known.

Wilson's other two conspicuous appointments from Wall Street at first aroused great approval. After the collapse of the aircraft programme, he placed in charge of this work John D. Ryan, president of the Anaconda Copper Mining Company. The result was the immediate revitalizing of the department, although the war ended before Ryan had a chance to demonstrate his complete success. But perhaps the Wall Street man who scored the greatest triumph was Charles M. Schwab. Wilson experimented disastrously for more than a year with the Shipping Board, the repeated failures of which almost disheartened the American people and their allies. All this time there was one man, and one man only, ideally fitted for the task. Finally Wilson sent for the head of the Bethlehem Steel Company. At first Schwab said that it would be utterly impossible for him to undertake the work. Being pressed for an explanation, he declared that he was no politician; the drastic reorganization he would insist on making would be extremely unpopular. The President immediately told him that he should have an absolutely free hand and that he would be required to do only one thing — build ships. Schwab still hesitated; the first step he should take, he informed the President, would be to move the head offices of the Shipping Board from Washington to Philadelphia. "You can move them to Kalamazoo," the President is reported to have answered, "if by doing so you can build ships." This very satisfactory attitude persuaded Schwab to take charge, which he did with his characteristic enthusiasm and energy, and soon the vessels began to leave the ways in great numbers. It is hardly too much to say that Schwab's appointment sealed the fate of submarine warfare.

Thus Wall Street emerged from the war with greatly enhanced prestige. Without the financial support which it placed at the Government's disposal, without the mammoth industrial organization which America had developed since 1865, the United States would have counted for little in the struggle.

APPENDIX

EXTRACTS FROM CHAPTER THREE OF THE REPORT OF THE COMMITTEE APPOINTED PURSUANT TO HOUSE RESOLUTIONS 429 AND 504 TO INVESTIGATE THE CONCENTRATION OF CONTROL OF MONEY AND CREDIT (HOUSE REPORT NO. 1593, 62D CONGRESS, 3D SESSION, 1913)

Section 3 — Processes of Concentration

THIS increased concentration of control of money and credit has been effected principally as follows:

First, through consolidations of competitive or potentially competitive banks and trust companies, which consolidations in turn have recently been brought under sympathetic management.

Second, through the same powerful interests becoming large stockholders in potentially competitive banks and trust companies. This is the simplest way of acquiring control, but since it requires the largest investment of capital, it is the least used, although the recent investments in that direction for that apparent purpose amount to tens of millions of dollars in present market values.

Third, through the confederation of potentially competitive banks and trust companies by means of the system of interlocking directorates.

Fourth, through the influence which the more powerful banking houses, banks, and trust companies have secured in the management of insurance companies, railroads, producing and trading corporations, and public utility corporations, by means of stockholdings, voting trusts, fiscal agency contracts, or representation upon their boards of directors, or through supplying the money requirements of railway, industrial, and public utilities corporations and thereby being enabled to participate in the determination of their financial and business policies.

Fifth, through partnership or joint account arrangements between a few of the leading banking houses, banks, and trust companies in the purchase of security issues of the great interstate corporations, accompanied by understandings of recent growth — sometimes called "banking ethics" — which have had the effect of effectually destroying competition between such banking houses, banks, and trust companies in the struggle for business or in the purchase and sale of large issues of such securities.

Section 4 — Agents of Concentration

It is a fair deduction from the testimony that the most active agents in forwarding and bringing about the concentration of control of money and credit through one or another of the processes above described have been and are:

J. P. Morgan & Co.
First National Bank of New York.
National City Bank of New York.
Lee, Higginson & Co., of Boston and New York.
Kidder, Peabody & Co., of Boston and New York.
Kuhn, Loeb & Co.

.   .   .   .

Section 11 — Interrelations of Members of the Group

Morgan & Co. and First National Bank. — Mr. Morgan, head of the firm of Morgan & Co., of New York, and Drexel & Co., of Philadelphia, and Mr. Baker, head officer and dominant power in the First National Bank since shortly after its organization, have been close friends and business associates from almost the time they began business. Mr. Morgan testifying as to their relations, said (p. 1034):

Q. You and Mr. Baker have been old and close friends and associates for many years, have you not?

A. For a great many years; yes.

Q. Almost since you began business?

A. Well, since 1873, at least.

Q. During that time your house has been of great aid to the First National Bank in building up their great prosperity and they have been of great aid to you?

A. I hope so.

Q. That is the fact, is it not?

A. That is the fact, I think.

Q. During that period you have made many purchases of securities jointly and many joint issues of securities, have you not?

A. Yes, sir.

Before becoming partners in Morgan & Co., Mr. Davison and Mr. Lamont, two of the most active members of the firm, were vice presidents of the First National Bank, and still remain directors.

Next to Mr. Baker, Morgan & Co. is the largest stockholder of the First National, owning 14,500 shares, making the combined holdings of Mr. Baker and his son and Morgan & Co. about 40,000 shares out of 100,000 outstanding — a joint investment, based on the market value, of $41,000,000 in this one institution.

Three of the Morgan partners — Mr. Morgan himself, Mr. Davison, and Mr. Lamont — are directors of the First National, and Mr. Morgan is a member of the executive committee of four, which has not, however, been active and has rarely met.

The First National has been associated with Morgan & Co. in the control of the Bankers Trust Co. As before stated, when the company was organized, its entire capital stock was vested in George W. Perkins, H. P. Davison, and Daniel G. Reid as voting trustees. Mr. Perkins was then a Morgan partner and Mr. Davison and Mr. Reid were, respectively, vice president and a large stockholder of the First National. Mr. Davison, who has since become a Morgan partner, and Mr. Reid have continued as such trustees. Mr. Perkins has been succeeded by the attorney of the company, who is also Mr. Davison's personal counsel. Mr. Davison and Mr. Lamont, of the Morgan firm, and Mr. Hine, president, Mr. Norton, vice president, and Mr. Hepburn, member of the executive committee of the First National, are codirectors of the Bankers Trust Co., Mr. Hine being also a member of its executive committee.

The First National likewise has been associated with Morgan & Co. in the control of the Guaranty Trust Co., Mr. Baker of the former being joined with Mr. Davison and Mr. Porter of the latter as voting trustees.

In the Astor Trust Co., controlled by Morgan & Co. through the Bankers Trust Co., Mr. Baker and Mr. Hine, chief officers of the First National, are directors.

In the Liberty National Bank, controlled by Morgan

& Co. through the Bankers Trust Co., Mr. Hine is also a director.

Since its organization in 1894, Mr. Morgan and Mr. Baker have been associated as voting trustees in the control of the Southern Railway, of which, also, Morgan & Co. and the First Security Co. are stockholders, and Mr. Steele of the former and George F. Baker, Jr., and H. C. Fahnestock of the First National are directors.

Mr. Morgan and Mr. Baker are also associated as voting trustees in the control of the Chicago Great Western Railway.

Mr. Morgan and Mr. Baker are further associated as directors and members of the executive committee of the New York Central Lines and as directors of the New York, New Haven & Hartford Railroad and the Pullman Co.

At Mr. Morgan's request, Mr. Baker became and has remained a director and member of the finance committee of the United States Steel Corporation, which, as previously shown, was organized and always has been dominated by the former. At the request of Mr. Perkins, who, as a partner in Morgan & Co., was active in organizing the International Harvester Co., Mr. Baker became a director of that company, resigning only recently.

Mr. Stotesbury, of Morgan & Co., and Mr. Baker are associated as voting trustees in the control of the William Cramp Ship & Engine Building Co.

In 1901 Mr. Baker and associates, coöperating with Mr. Morgan, transferred to Reading Co. a majority of the stock of the Central Railroad of New Jersey, thereby bringing under one control railroad systems transporting $33\frac{1}{3}$ per cent of the anthracite coal moving from the mines and coal companies owning or controlling 63 per cent of the entire anthracite deposits. (Baker, R., 1504, 1506, 1508.)

In the same year Mr. Baker coöperated with Mr. Morgan in transferring to the Northern Securities Co. controlling stock interests in the Northern Pacific and Great Northern Railways, competitive transcontinental systems.

One or more members of Morgan & Co. and one or more officers or directors of the First National are associated as codirectors in the following additional corporations, among others:

The Mutual Life Insurance Co. of New York;

The anthracite railroads, including the Reading, the Central of New Jersey, the Lehigh Valley, the Erie, the New York, Susquehanna & Western, and the New York, Ontario & Western;

The Northern Pacific Railway, in which also Mr. Steele, of Morgan & Co., and Mr. Baker, of the First National, are members of the executive committee;

Adams Express Co.;

American Telegraph & Telephone Co.; and

The Baldwin Locomotive Works.

But nothing demonstrates quite so clearly the close and continuing coöperation between Morgan & Co. and the First National Bank as their joint purchases and underwritings of corporate securities. Since 1903 they have purchased for their joint account, generally with other associates, 70 odd security issues of 30 different corporations, aggregating approximately $1,080,-000,000. (Ex. 213, R., 1895; Ex. 235, R., 2127.) A complete statement of such joint transactions in securities will be found in a subsequent part of this report.

It is thus seen that through stockholdings, inter-locking directors, partnership transactions, and other relations, Morgan & Co. and the First National Bank are locked together in a complete and enduring community of interest. Their relations in this regard are, indeed, a commonplace in the financial world. Thus, Mr. Schiff being asked whether he knew "the close relations between Messrs. Morgan and the First National Bank," replied "I do." (R., 1687.)

Morgan & Co., First National Bank, and National City Bank. — Mr. Stillman, as president, chairman of the board of directors and largest stockholder, for a long time has held a position of dominance in the National City Bank corresponding to Mr. Morgan's in his firm and Mr. Baker's in the First National Bank.

For many years while Morgan & Co. and the First National Bank were in close business union the National City Bank apparently occupied a position of independence. More recently, however, it has been drawn into the community of interest existing between the two first named, as is evidenced by a series of important transactions.

First. Within three or four years Morgan & Co. acquired $1,500,000 par value of the capital stock of the National City Bank, representing an investment at the stock's present market price of $6,000,000, and J. P. Morgan, Jr., became a director. (Morgan, R., 1036, 1075, 1076; Davison, R., 1879; Ex. 134-A.)

Second. In 1910 Mr. Morgan in conjunction with both Mr. Baker, his long-time associate, and Mr. Stillman, head of the National City Bank, purchased from Ryan and the Mr. Harriman estate $51,000, par value, of the stock of the Equitable Life Assurance Society, paying therefor what Mr. Ryan originally paid with interest at 5 per cent — about $3,000,000 — the investment yielding less than one-eighth of 1 per cent. Mr. Stillman and Mr. Baker each agreed to take a one-fourth interest in the purchase if requested to do so by Mr. Morgan. No such request has yet been made by him.

No sufficient reason has been given for this transaction, nor does any suggest itself, unless it was the desire of these gentlemen to control the investment of the $504,000,000 of assets of this company, or the disposition of the bank and trust company stocks which it held and was compelled by law to sell within a stated time. Mr. Morgan was interrogated as follows on this subject (R., 1068, 1069, 1071):

Q. You may explain, if you care to, Mr. Morgan, why you bought from Messrs. Ryan and Harriman $51,000 par value of stock that paid only $3710 a year, for approximately $3,000,000, that could yield you only one-eighth or one-ninth of 1 per cent.

A. Because I thought it was a desirable thing for the situation to do that.

Q. That is very general, Mr. Morgan, when you speak of the situation. Was not that stock safe enough in Mr. Ryan's hands?

A. I suppose it was. I thought it was greatly improved by being in the hands of myself and these two gentlemen, provided I asked them to do so.

Q. How would that improve the situation over the situation that existed when Mr. Ryan and Mr. Harriman held the stock?

A. Mr. Ryan did not have it alone.

Q. Yes; but do you not know that Mr. Ryan originally bought it alone and Mr. Harriman insisted on having him give him half?

A. I thought if he could pay for it that price I could. I thought that was a fair price.

Q. You thought it was good business, did you?

A. Yes.

Q. You thought it was good business to buy a stock that paid only one-ninth or one-tenth of 1 per cent a year?

A. I thought so.

Q. The normal rate of interest that you can earn on money is about 5 per cent, is it not?

A. Not always; no.

Q. I say, ordinarily.

A. I am not talking about it as a question of money.

Q. The normal rate of interest would be from 4 to 5 per cent, ordinarily, would it not?

A. Well?

Q. Where is the good business, then, in buying a security that only pays one-ninth of 1 per cent?

A. Because I thought it was better there than it was where it was. That is all.

Q. Was anything the matter with it in the hands of Mr. Ryan?

A. Nothing.

Q. In what respect would it be better where it is than with him?

A. That is the way it struck me.

Q. Is that all you have to say about it?

A. That is all I have to say about it.

Q. You care to make no other explanation about it?

A. No.

.   .   .   .

Q. I do not understand why you bought this company.

A. For the very reason that I thought it was the thing to do, as I said.

Q. But that does not explain anything.

A. That is the only reason I can give.

Q. It was the thing to do for whom?

A. That is the only reason I can give. That is the only reason I have, in other words. I am not trying to keep anything back, you understand.

Q. I understand. In other words, you have no reason at all?

A. That is the way you look at it. I think it is a very good reason.

Mr. Baker was asked the following questions (R., 1466, 1467, 1469, 1470, 1535):

Q. Coming, now, to this transaction of the Equitable Life. You remember when Mr. Morgan acquired the control from Messrs. Ryan and Harriman, do you not?

A. Yes, sir.

Q. When was it?

A. I could not tell you that date.

Q. It was in 1910, was it not.

A. If that is what you have in your record there, that is correct, I suppose.

Q. I think that is correct. Is that your recollection?

A. No; it is not my recollection; but it is on the record there.

Q. What is your recollection?

A. I know it was two or three years ago. That is all.

Q. At the time Mr. Morgan acquired the interest

in the Equitable, did he come with you?

A. Yes, sir.

Q. And with Mr. Stillman?

A. Yes.

. . . .

Q. . . . I want to ask you further concerning this Equitable Life transaction. Do I correctly understand that at the time Mr. Morgan made the purchase you and Mr. Stillman committed yourselves to take part of it?

A. That was done so informally ——

Q. (interrupting). Did you?

A. Yes; I will say we did.

Q. You were consulted before it was done and you agreed to take a part of it?

A. Yes.

Q. Then, following that, about a year later, you were asked to write this letter, were you not, confirming that arrangement?

A. Yes. Mr. J. P. Morgan, Jr., wrote me a letter and I put my initials at the bottom, saying it was so, or something of that kind.

. . . .

Q. Referring back, now, to the talk you say you had with Mr. Morgan and Mr. Stillman about the purchase of the Equitable stock; before it was purchased, what reason did Mr. Morgan give for wanting to take that stock from Mr. Ryan?

A. I can not remember that he gave any special reason, except that he thought it would be a good thing to be in his hands.

Q. When he said he thought it would be a good thing to be in his hands, rather than in the hands of Mr.

Ryan, what did you understand that to mean?

A. I did not understand that to mean much of anything. I did not take much interest in it.

Third, about a year later Mr. Stillman and Mr. Baker, pursuant to an understanding between them and J. P. Morgan & Co., purchased approximately one-half of the holdings of the Mutual and Equitable Life insurance companies in the stock of the National Bank of Commerce, amounting altogether to some 42,200 shares. Mr. Baker being a member of the finance committee of the Mutual, it was arranged that he should purchase the Equitable's stock — about 15,250 shares — and Mr. Stillman the Mutual's. Pursuant to the understanding, Mr. Stillman turned over 10,000 shares to Morgan & Co., who already owned 7000 shares. Mr. Baker kept 5000 shares, turned over 5000 to the First Security Co., and distributed the rest among various persons; 3000 shares were allotted by Mr. Stillman and Mr. Baker to Kuhn, Loeb & Co.

Mr. Baker testified as follows regarding this transaction (R., 1463, 1464):

Q. Was the purchase of that stock the result of an understanding between you and him and others?

A. Yes, sir.

Q. Who were the others?

A. Some of the people at Mr. Morgan's.

Q. Who?

A. I can not remember whether it was Mr. Morgan himself, or Jack — I mean Mr. J. P. Morgan, Jr. — or some others; I do not remember.

Q. Then the purchase altogether amounted to about 42,200 shares, did it not, from the two companies?

A. Yes.

Q. What arrangement was there as to the distribution of that stock; how it should be distributed between Messrs. Morgan and Stillman and yourself?

A. I can not remember that there was any in particular. I disposed of mine as I have told you, and that is as near as I can remember. I can account for the bulk of it.

Q. Was there or was there not talk about the distribution of that 42,200 shares?

A. There may have been, but I do not remember.

Q. You do not remember whether there was or not?

A. No, sir.

Q. And you can not tell what Messrs. Morgan & Co. agreed to take before the stock was bought?

A. I do not know whether they agreed to take any. I think Mr. Morgan took 10,000 shares, probably, from Mr. Stillman.

Q. Before you bought the stock between you, these three interests, was there not some understanding, and if so, what was it, as to the way it should be divided up?

A. Possibly there was, but I do not remember clearly enough to answer the question intelligently to you. I am willing to admit, if it is of any interest to the committee, that there was an understanding and that we were to take it for joint account.

Q. The committee would rather not have any admissions that do not agree with your recollection, if you have no recollection of it at all.

A. I have not a definite enough recollection to state under oath.

Q. Is it your impression that there was an understanding that it was purchased for joint account?

A. Yes.

Q. Between those three interests?

A. Yes; that it would be divided. I do not think they were for joint account.

The National City Bank, the First National, and Morgan & Co. now have two representatives each on the board of directors of the National Bank of Commerce — Mr. Vanderlip, president, and Mr. Simonson, vice president, of the first named; Mr. Baker, chairman of the board, and Mr. Hine, president of the second; and H. P. Davison and J. P. Morgan, Jr., of the last; whilst six of its finance committee of nine (it has no executive committee) consist of Mr. Vanderlip and Mr. Simonson of the National City Bank, Mr. Hine of the First National, Mr. Wiggin, president of the Chase National, which, as appeared above, has for some years been controlled by the First National, and Mr. Davison and Mr. J. P. Morgan, Jr., of J. P. Morgan & Co.

Fourth, during the same period in which occurred the three transactions just described — that is, within the last four years — the National City Bank, the First National, and Morgan & Co. (excluding issues in which there were other parties to the joint account) have purchased or underwritten in joint account thirty-six security issues (including the impending issue of the Interborough Rapid Transit Co.) amounting to $484,-456,000 and they, with other associates, thirty-one additional issues amounting to $548,027,000, making in all sixty-seven issues aggregating over $1,000,000,000 in which the First National, the National City Bank, and Morgan & Co. were joint purchasers or underwriters. Further, in the same period, the National

City Bank and Morgan & Co. and other associates, not including the First National, have purchased or underwritten in joint account twenty security issues aggregating $333,385,000. On the other hand, in the ten years prior to 1908 the National City Bank joined with Morgan & Co. in but one purchase or underwriting of securities and with the First National in not one.

The acquisition by Morgan & Co. of a large block of stock of the National City Bank with representation upon its board of directors, and the transactions that followed, in which those two institutions and the First National Bank were joined, as above set forth, show a unison of interest and a continuity of coöperation between the three such as for many years previously had existed between two of them — Morgan & Co. and the First National.

Combined power of Morgan & Co., the First National, and National City Banks. — In earlier pages of the report the power of these three great banks was separately set forth. It is now appropriate to consider their combined power as one group.

First, as regards banking resources:

The resources of Morgan & Co. are unknown; its deposits are $163,000,000. The resources of the First National Bank are $150,000,000 and those of its appendage, the First Security Co., at a very low estimate, $35,000,000. The resources of the National City Bank are $274,000,000; those of its appendage, the National City Co., are unknown, though the capital of the latter is alone $10,000,000. Thus, leaving out of account the very considerable part which is unknown, the institutions composing this group have resources of upward of

$632,000,000, aside from the vast individual resources of Messrs. Morgan, Baker, and Stillman.

Further, as heretofore shown, the members of this group, through stockholdings, voting trusts, interlocking directorates, and other relations, have become in some cases the absolutely dominant factor, in others the most important single factor, in the control of the following banks and trust companies in the city of New York:

(a)	Bankers Trust Co., resources.....	$205,000,000
(b)	Guaranty Trust Co., resources....	232,000,000
(c)	Astor Trust Co., resources.......	27,000,000
(d)	National Bank of Commerce, resources....................	190,000,000
(e)	Liberty National Bank, resources.	29,000,000
(f)	Chase National Bank, resources....	150,000,000
(g)	Farmers Loan & Trust Co., resources.....................	135,000,000
in all, 7, with total resources of.......		968,000,000
which, added to the known resources of members of the group themselves, makes.........................		$1,600,000,000
as the aggregate of known banking resources in the city of New York under their control or influence.		
If there be added also the resources of the Equitable Life Assurance Society controlled through stock ownership of J. P. Morgan.................		504,000,000
the amount becomes...............		$2,104,000,000

Second, as regards the greater transportation systems.

(a) Adams Express Co.: Members of the group have two representatives in the directorate of this company.

(b) Anthracite coal carriers: With the exception of the Pennsylvania and the Delaware & Hudson, the Reading, the Central of New Jersey (a majority of whose stock is owned by the Reading), the Lehigh Valley, the Delaware, Lackawanna & Western, the Erie (controlling the New York, Susquehanna & Western), and the New York, Ontario & Western, afford the only transportation outlets from the anthracite coal fields. As before stated, they transport 80 per cent of the output moving from the mines and own and control 88 per cent of the entire deposits. The Reading, as now organized, is the creation of a member of this banking group — Morgan & Co. One or more members of the group are stockholders in that system and have two representatives in its directorate; are stockholders of the Central of New Jersey and have four representatives in its directorate; are stockholders of the Lehigh Valley and have four representatives in its directorate; are stockholders of the Delaware, Lackawanna & Western and have nine representatives in its directorate; are stockholders of the Erie and have four representatives in its directorate; have two representatives in the directorate of the New York, Ontario & Western; and have purchased or marketed practically all security issues made by these railroads in recent years.

(c) Atchison, Topeka & Santa Fe Railway: One or more members of the group are stockholders and have two representatives in the directorate of the company; and since 1907 have purchased or procured the marketing of its security issues to the amount of $107,244,000.

(d) Chesapeake & Ohio Railway: Members of the group have two directors in common with this company, and since 1907, in association with others, have purchased or procured the marketing of its security issues to the amount of $85,000,000.

(e) Chicago Great Western Railway: Members of

the group absolutely control this system through a voting trust.

(*f*) Chicago, Milwaukee & St. Paul Railway: Members of the group have three directors or officers in common with this company, and since 1909, in association with others, have purchased or procured the marketing of its security issues to the amount of $112,000,000.

(*g*) Chicago & Northwestern Railway: Members of the group have three directors in common with this company, and since 1909, in association with others, have purchased or procured the marketing of its security issues to the amount of $31,250,000.

(*h*) Chicago, Rock Island & Pacific Railway: Members of the group have four directors in common with this company.

(*i*) Great Northern Railway: One or more members of the group are stockholders of and have marketed the only issue of bonds made by this company.

(*j*) International Mercantile Marine Co.: A member of the group organized this company, is a stockholder, dominates it through a voting trust, and markets its securities.

(*k*) New York Central Lines: One or more members of the group are stockholders and have four representatives in the directorate of the company, and since 1907 have purchased from or marketed for it and its principal subsidiaries security issues to the extent of $343,000,000, one member of the group being the company's sole fiscal agent.

(*l*) New York, New Haven & Hartford Railroad: One or more members of the group are stockholders and have three representatives in the directorate of the company, and since 1907 have purchased from or marketed for it and its principal subsidiaries security issues in excess of $150,000,000, one member of the group being the company's sole fiscal agent.

(m) Northern Pacific Railway: One member of the group organized this company and is its fiscal agent, and one or more members are stockholders and have six representatives in its directorate and three in its executive committee.

(n) Southern Railway: Through a voting trust, members of the group have absolutely controlled this company since its reorganization in 1894.

(o) Southern Pacific Co.: Until its separation from the Union Pacific, lately ordered by the Supreme Court of the United States, members of the group had three directors in common with this company.

(p) Union Pacific Railroad: Members of the group have three directors in common with this company.

Third, as regards the greater producing and trading corporations.

(a) Amalgamated Copper Co.: One member of the group took part in the organization of the company, still has one leading director in common with it, and markets its securities.

(b) American Can Co.: Members of the group have two directors in common with this company.

(c) J. I. Case Threshing Machine Co.: The president of one member of the group is a voting trustee of this company and the group also has one representative in its directorate and markets its securities.

(d) William Cramp Ship & Engine Building Co.: Members of the group absolutely control this company through a voting trust.

(*e*) General Electric Co.: A member of the group was one of the organizers of the company, is a stockholder, and has always had two representatives in its directorate, and markets its securities.

(*f*) International Harvester Co.: A member of the group organized the company, named its directorate and the chairman of its finance committee, directed its management through a voting trust, is a stockholder, and markets its securities.

(*g*) Lackawanna Steel Co.: Members of the group have four directors in common with the company and, with associates, marketed its last issue of securities.

(*h*) Pullman Co.: The group has two representatives, Mr. Morgan and Mr. Baker, in the directorate of this company.

(*i*) United States Steel Corporation: A member of the group organized this company, named its directorate, and the chairman of its finance committee (which also has the powers of an executive committee) is its sole fiscal agent and a stockholder, and has always controlled its management.

Fourth, as regards the great public utility corporations.

(*a*) American Telephone & Telegraph Co.: One or more members of the group are stockholders, have three representatives in its directorate, and since 1906, with other associates, have marketed for it and its subsidiaries security issues in excess of $300,000,000.

(*b*) Chicago Elevated Railways: A member of the group has two officers or directors in common with the company, and in conjunction with others marketed for it in 1911 security issues amounting to $66,000,000.

(*c*) Consolidated Gas Co. of New York: Members

of the group control this company through majority representation on its directorate.

(d) Hudson & Manhattan Railroad: One or more members of the group marketed and have large interests in the securities of this company, though its debt is now being adjusted by Kuhn, Loeb & Co.

(e) Interborough Rapid Transit Co. of New York: A member of the group is the banker of this company, and the group has agreed to market its impending bond issue of $170,000,000.

(f) Philadelphia Rapid Transit Co.: Members of the group have two representatives in the directorate of this company.

(g) Western Union Telegraph Co.: Members of the group have seven representatives in the directorate of this company.

Summary of directorships held by these members of the group. — Exhibit 134-B . . . shows the combined directorships in the more important enterprises held by Morgan & Co., the First National Bank, the National City Bank, and the Bankers and Guaranty Trust Cos., which latter two, as previously shown, are absolutely controlled by Morgan & Co. through voting trusts. It appears here that firm members or directors of these institutions together hold:

One hundred and eighteen directorships in thirty-four banks and trust companies having total resources of $2,679,000,000 and total deposits of $1,983,000,000.

Thirty directorships in ten insurance companies having total assets of $2,293,000,000.

One hundred and five directorships in thirty-two transportation systems having a total capitalization of

$11,784,000,000 and a total mileage (excluding express companies and steamship lines) of 150,200.

Sixty-three directorships in twenty-four producing and trading corporations having a total capitalization of $3,339,000,000.

Twenty-five directorships in twelve public utility corporations having a total capitalization of $2,150,000,000.

In all, 341 directorships in 112 corporations having aggregate resources or capitalization of $22,245,000,000.

The members of the firm of J. P. Morgan & Co. hold seventy-two directorships in forty-seven of the greater corporations; George F. Baker, chairman of the board, F. L. Hine, president, and George F. Baker, Jr., and C. D. Norton, vice presidents, of the First National Bank of New York hold forty-six directorships in thirty-seven of the greater corporations; and James Stillman, chairman of the board, Frank A. Vanderlip, president, and Samuel McRoberts, J. T. Talbert, W. A. Simonson, vice presidents, of the National City Bank of New York, hold thirty-two directorships in twenty-six of the greater corporations; making in all for these members of the group 150 directorships in 110 of the greater corporations.

The affiliations of these and other banking institutions with the larger railroad, industrial, and public utility corporations and banks, trust companies, and insurance companies of the United States, are shown in graphic form in two diagrams which are in evidence and are attached to this report as Appendices F and G

Relations between Morgan & Co., First National Bank, National City Bank, Lee Higginson & Co., Kidder, Peabody & Co., and Kuhn, Loeb & Co. — Besides the group

composed of Morgan & Co. and the First National
Bank and the National City Bank, the principal banking agencies through which the greater corporate enterprises of the United States obtain capital for their
operations are the international banking firms of Kuhn,
Loeb & Co., of New York, and Kidder, Peabody & Co.
and Lee Higginson & Co., of Boston and New York.

While it does not appear that these three last-named
houses are affiliated with the group consisting of the
first three in so definite and permanent a form of alliance
as that existing between the latter, it is established that
as issuing houses they do not as a rule act independently in purchasing security issues but rather in unison and coöperation with one or more members of that
group, with the result that in the vastly important
service of arranging credits for the great commercial
enterprises of the country there is no competition or
rivalry between those dominating that field, but vir-
tually a monopoly, the terms of which the borrowing
corporations must accept.

The full extent to which they participate in one
another's issues does not appear, owing to the absence
of data as to the names of underwriters, other than in
strictly joint-account transactions of the issues of securities made by Messrs. Morgan & Co., Kuhn, Loeb & Co.,
the First National Bank, and the National City Bank.
The distinction between the cases in which one of the
banks or banking houses assumes the relation of an
underwriter of an issue of securities made by one of the
others and that in which they act in joint account is
that in the former case underwriters do not share in the
primary bankers' profit, but insure the former against
loss, while in the case of a joint account they are part-

ners and as such share in the original risks and profits.

The course of business is for the house acquiring from a corporation the right of purchasing or underwriting an issue of its securities to offer participations in the purchase or underwriting to one or more of the associates named. Taking as an illustration the latest issue of the American Telephone & Telegraph Co., the method of procedure is thus described in the testimony of Mr. Schiff (R., 1664):

Q. And is there not an issue now in course of offer to the public of American Telephone & Telegraph bonds?

A. There is.

Q. Advertised in the last few days?

A. In course of offer to stockholders; not to the public.

Q. They are in course of offer to the stockholders and if the stockholders do not take them, are they then to be offered to the public?

A. Then the underwriting syndicate will have to take them, and whether they will offer them to the public or not I do not know.

Q. But it is an issue that is publicly offered to the stockholders?

A. It is going to be publicly offered to the stockholders.

Q. What is the amount of that issue?

A. I believe it is between $60,000,000 and $70,000,000.

Q. It is $67,000,000, is it not?

A. It may be $67,000,000; I do not recall.

Q. Is that a joint-account transaction between Morgan, Kidder, Peabody, and yourselves?

A. It is a joint account transaction between

Morgan's, First National Bank, the National City Bank, Kidder, Peabody & Co., and Baring Bros., and ourselves.

Q. Baring Bros., of London?

A. Yes.

Q. Take that as an illustration; who made the deal with the company?

A. I believe J. P. Morgan & Co.

Q. And they invited you to participate on joint account with these other houses?

A. They did.

. . . .

It was admitted by Mr. Davison, of Morgan & Co., and other bankers that the practice of banking houses becoming in effect partners in the purchasing and underwriting of securities instead of acting independently of one another is a development of recent years.

Mr. Davison testified as follows (R., 1854, 1855).

Q. Recently, within the last few years, many of the issues of J. P. Morgan & Co. have been made jointly with the First National Bank and the National City Bank, have they not?

A. Yes.

Q. And many with Lee-Higginson and with western bankers?

A. No; not very many with the western bankers. As a matter of fact, I recall very few with the western bankers. We have made them occasionally with Lee-Higginson and with other houses.

Q. You have made them very largely with Lee-Higginson?

A. It is comparative. I do not think we have, very largely.

Q. But your main joint-account transactions are with the City Bank and the First National Bank?

A. I think they have been.

Q. Is it not a fact that in previous years you made the issues largely alone, prior to five years ago?

A. I think more largely alone; yes, sir. They were smaller in character.

Q. Within what length of time has it been that J. P. Morgan & Co. have done most of their issuing business in joint account? Has it been within your time?

A. No; I think it was a little before my time.

Q. You think it started a little before your time?

A. I think it started a little before my time. In fact, the evidence shows that it did.

Mr. Schiff said (R., 1688):

Q. Don't you know that most of the Morgan issues in the past few years have been made jointly; that is, that the City Bank has participated in them with the First National?

A. I do.

Mr. Schiff is a director of the City Bank.

It will be noticed that Mr. Davison advances the great size of present-day security issues in explanation of why banking houses now purchase such issues in combination or for joint account instead of independently, as formerly. The fact is, however, . . . that not only are small issues still very frequent, but they are purchased in concert as regularly as the larger issues. Of the issues since 1907 . . . purchased or underwritten by two or more of the banking houses there named acting together, about ninety were for $5,000,000 and less, while an additional sixty were for amounts between $5,000,000 and $10,000,000. It also appears that forty-five of such issues for $5,000,000 and less, most of them made since 1909, were purchased or underwritten by Morgan & Co. in conjunction with associates.

Of course we do not suggest that banking houses may not on particular occasions join in purchasing or underwriting an issue of securities and yet remain entirely independent and free to compete with each other generally in the purchase of security issues. But where a group of such banking houses, pursuant to a settled policy, regularly purchase these issues in concert, competition amongst them in this vastly important commercial function is effectually suppressed. And that is the situation in this country. No less an authority than Mr. Baker admitted as much (R., 1542, 1543):

Q. But among these banking houses that we have named is there not a strong and continuous community of interest in the purchase and sale of securities?

A. I think there is. We have always tried to deal with our friends rather than with people we do not know.

Q. It is a good deal better to deal with your friends and split it up than it is to compete for the securities?

A. Not necessarily.

Q. That is what happens, is it not?

A. Oh, I do not think so to any great extent.

Q. Have you ever competed for any securities with Morgan & Co. in the last five years? If so, give us the name of them.

A. I do not know that we have competed with them.

Q. You divide with them, do you not? You give them a part of the issues when you have it?

A. We are apt to.

Q. And if they take a security they give you a part

of the issue, do they not?

A. Yes.

Q. That is what is known as the modern system of coöperation and combination as against the antique system of competition, is it not?

A. That is rather a long name for me.

Q. You understand the question. I would like to have you answer it.

A. I never heard it called in that way before.

Q. How would you call it?

A. I would not call it at all.

Q. You know what coöperation is, do you not?

A. Yes.

Q. Is that not coöperation as against competition? That is the modern system of coöperation as against the archaic system of competition, is it not?

A. I do not understand how you state that.

Q. That is right, is it not?

A. All right; yes.

Q. And that has been found to work very well, has it not?

A. I think so.

Q. For the bankers?

A. Yes; and for others, too.

Moreover, the banking houses which have joined in the plan of coöperation comprise the principal mediums through which the greater corporations of the country obtain their supplies of capital.

The charge for capital, which, of course, enters universally into the prices of commodities and of service, is thus in effect determined by agreement amongst those supplying it, and not under the check of competition. If there be any virtue in the principle of competition, certainly any plan or arrangement which prevents its operation in the performance of so fundamental a commercial function as the supplying of capital is peculiarly injurious.

The possibility of competition between these banking houses in the purchase of securities is further removed by the understanding amongst them and others that one will not seek by offering better terms to take away from another a customer which it has theretofore served, and by the corollary of this, namely, that where given bankers have once satisfactorily united in bringing out an issue of a corporation they shall also join in bringing out any subsequent issue of the same corporation. This is described as a principle of banking ethics. It is thus stated by Mr. Hine, president of the First National Bank of New York (R., 2045, 2046):

Q. Recently your bank made an issue, jointly with J. P. Morgan & Co. and the National City Bank, of Chicago & Western Indiana Railway bonds, of ten millions, did it not?

A. Notes.

Q. Ten millions of notes, yes. Why was it necessary that three great banking houses should join in an issue of that kind?

A. I do not know of any reason.

Q. Was it not because they had been jointly interested in previous issues of the same company?

A. I do not know that it was.

Q. Had they been jointly interested in previous issues?

A. I think they had.

Q. Is it or is it not the custom when banking houses

are interested or become interested in one kind of issues of a company that they retain that interest in other issues?

A. Often it is so.

Q. That is part of the banking ethics, is it not?

A. Yes, I would say it is; on satisfactory terms.

Q. Is it another rule of banking ethics that bankers shall not interfere with one another's customers?

A. The same ethics obtain in banking that obtain in the legal profession and in the medical profession as to infringing upon the preserves of others.

Q. Well, what are the ethics in the banking profession as to trespassing upon the preserves of others?

A. If you will tell me what the ethics are in the legal world, I will answer your question.

Q. No; I would rather have you tell me the ethics in the world with which you are acquainted.

A. I can not state the matter any better than you have. It is the custom — I am not dealing in ethics.

Q. What is the custom among bankers and banking houses as to any one interfering with another's customer in business?

A. I do not know whether there is any custom. I think it is considered unprofessional.

Q. Unbusinesslike?

A. And not in good form according to the highest principles of business practice.

Q. Is it not in accordance with banking ethics to interfere with or take customers away from firms; to take customers who have been doing business with some other banking house?

A. I think that is ordinarily considered high-minded practice not to do so.

Mr. Davison testifying on the same subject said (R., 1858, 1859):

Q. Then you know of these three instances — the Chicago & Western Indiana Railway Co., the Kansas City Terminal Co., and the New York Central, all made within a few weeks jointly with other banking houses — those we have been discussing. Is there any rule or custom among bankers that where they make one issue of a company or are interested together in one issue they remain interested in subsequent issues?

A. For the same company?

Q. Yes.

A. As a matter of practice, if it was satisfactory in every particular, I should say it was the custom; yes. It is a matter of banking ethics.

Q. A matter of banking ethics?

A. I should say so; yes.

Q. If either one of the three thereafter gets an issue of that company it is a matter of banking ethics that it is for joint account, is it?

A. I should say that the natural way of handling that business would be to have it go to the parties who handled it before, if it were satisfactorily handled; yes.

Q. You mean if they have not had any differences or disagreements between themselves?

A. Yes, if it was satisfactorily handled.

Q. Have you not within the last few weeks also taken an issue of $67,000,000 of American Telephone & Telegraph Co. bonds jointly with Lee-Higginson and other banking houses?

A. No.

Q. You participated with them in that issue?

A. Excuse me, I was going to answer your question.

I think with others, not including Lee-Higginson & Co.
as principals, but with Kidder, Peabody & Co., the
First National, the National City Bank, Baring Bros.
& Co. (Ltd.), of London, and Morgan-Grenfell (Ltd.),
of London, we have underwritten an issue of $67,000,000
of American Telephone & Telegraph Co. bonds.

Q. Are they the same parties ——

A. I beg your pardon — and Kuhn, Loeb & Co.

Q. Are they the same bankers or banking houses
with which you had previously underwritten issues of
the American Telephone & Telegraph Co.?

A. Exactly; and that is a complete answer to your
question.

Q. You have together underwritten, I think, $150,-
000,000 of those bonds, have you not?

A. That is my recollection.

Q. So that the same rule of banking ethics required
the same disposition of this issue as of the others?

A. I would not say it required it.

Q. It resulted in it?

A. It resulted in it, exactly.

Q. As a matter of fact, in business morals it would
require it.

A. It would require it if everything was properly
and satisfactorily handled, and there were no other
factors in the situation which might make it inexpe-
dient. The situation, when a transaction comes up
always governs.

Mr. Schiff was more guarded in his statement of the
practice (R., 1666, 1668, 1669):

Q. And you would not, for instance, if you knew
the Southern Railway was going to make an issue of

securities, be willing to bid on them, would you?

A. We would not.

Q. In other words, these houses have their recognized clients, have they not?

A. To some extent.

Q. And is it not also recognized that they are their clients and that they are not to be interfered with?

A. I think that is going a bit too far, because there is very frequently interference or attempted interference.

Q. Has there ever been any interference with your exclusively handling the issues of the Union Pacific Railroad in the last ten years?

A. I do not think so.

.   .   .   .

Q. Have you any instance in mind in which in the last five years you have invaded the field of Messrs. Morgan & Co. or they have invaded yours?

A. I have not.

Q. Or have you in mind any instance in which you have invaded the field of the National City Bank or the First National Bank, or in which they have invaded yours?

A. As to the First National Bank, I know we have not. As to the National City Bank I can not say for certain. I think they would do business to a certain extent even where we are considered the agents, and we would do certain business where they are considered the agents; not to a large extent.

Q. Is not that where the corporation is a customer of both of you? Is not that the only case in which the corporation is claimed to be or regarded as a customer of both of you or either of you?

A. It is in cases where a corporation is regarded as a

customer of neither.

Q. That is, in a case in which the field happens to be open?

A. Yes.

This custom, by whatever name it be called, and the practice of these great banking houses which it supplements of purchasing security issues in concert and not independently can not have any other effect than the suppression of competition in the purchasing of such securities, and the creation of a combination or community of interest which may grant or withhold credit as it wills and whose terms borrowing corporations must accept.

Undue concentration admitted. — Mr. Reynolds, president of the Continental & Commercial National Bank of Chicago, was outspoken in the view that concentration of control of banking resources has already gone so far as to be a menace to the country (R., 1654, 1655):

Q. I suppose, Mr. Reynolds, that as president of a great bank you have kept in touch with the very recent trend toward concentration and control of money and credit in the East?

A. Yes, sir; I have been constantly reminded of it in the last year or so.

Q. You know the extent to which it has gone in the last few years?

A. I have a general knowledge of it; yes, sir.

Q. Do you or not know the effect that has on the marketing of securities of a great railroad and other interstate corporations, and the trend of concentration brought about through the concentration of this money and credit?

A. I have read all that has been adduced at this

examination, and a great many other things, and my information in detail is very largely the result of this reading, rather than from personal experience.

Q. But you have information and knowledge of the conditions in New York, for instance, as between the great banking houses. That is a matter of personal knowledge?

A. Yes; I have a fairly general knowledge of that, I should say.

Q. What would you say as to that concentration of the control of money and credit being a menace to the country?

A. That involves a very deep question. Personally I am inclined to believe that an excess of power of any kind in the hands of a few men might properly be called a menace. I do not mean to say by that that the people who had that control and power have used it improperly. I do not mean to say that at all.

Q. Regardless of the way they have used it for the time being, the question is, is it not, as to the way they can use it?

A. I think a more wide distribution of the power of credit, if that is what you mean, would really be better in the long run.

Q. Taking the present situation as you find it, Mr. Reynolds, what is your judgment as to whether that situation is a menace?

A. I am inclined to think that the concentration, having gone to the extent it has, does constitute a menace. I wish again, however, to qualify that by saying that I do not mean to sit in judgment upon anybody who controls that, because I do not pretend to know whether they have used it fairly or honestly or otherwise.

Mr. Schiff also conceded rapid concentration of control of banking resources in New York in recent years, but he stated that it caused him no anxiety so far as the well-being of his own firm was concerned, as they were able to take care of themselves. We quote (R., 1686-1687, 1688):

Q. Have you been an interested observer of the concentration and control of money and credit in New York in the last few years?

A. I have.

Q. You have seen it grow very rapidly, have you not?

A. Yes.

Q. And you have seen it drift into fewer and fewer hands, have you not?

A. It has drifted into fewer and fewer corporations.

Q. And the concentration and control of those corporations has drifted into fewer hands, has it not?

A. I am not sure that it has done that.

Q. Do you know anything about it?

A. Well, I think the stockholding in different ——

Q. I say, do you know anything about it?

A. Not very closely.

Q. You have not watched it very closely?

A. I think stockholdings in most New York corporations are very well divided.

Q. We are not talking about stockholdings, but about practical control of management as distinguished from stockholding. You see the difference?

A. I see the difference.

Q. It is a very substantial difference, is it not?

A. Yes, sir.

Q. Now, confining yourself to the question of actual

practical control of the management of these great moneyed corporations, you have observed, have you not, a growing concentration of control?

A. I have.

Q. And has it been a subject of concern to you?

A. No; it has not.

. . . .

Q. You have been an interested onlooker in this concentration?

A. An observer; yes.

Q. And you have understood the possibility of its affecting you and your own sources of credit, have you not?

A. I have not been concerned in that.

Q. You do not require credit, then?

A. No.

Q. But you have considered its effect upon the small banking houses, not so fortunately situated as you, that do require credit?

A. Yes.

Q. Have you considered it?

A. Yes.

Q. And have you considered its effect on the ability of the smaller houses to grow and become great issuing houses?

A. Yes.

Finally, Mr. Baker, who is outranked only by Mr. Morgan, if at all, as a factor in the concentration of control of banking resources and credit into fewer and fewer hands in New York, frankly admitted that in his judgment the movement had gone far enough; that even if it stopped where it is the peril would be great if ambitious and not overscrupulous men should get into the places of power which have been created; and that therefore the safety of the existing system lies in the personnel of the men now in control. We quote from his illuminating testimony (R., 1567, 1568):

Q. I suppose you would see no harm, would you, in having the control of credit, as represented by the control of banks and trust companies, still further concentrated? Do you think that would be dangerous?

A. I think it has gone about far enough.

Q. You think it would be dangerous to go further?

A. It might not be dangerous, but still it has gone about far enough. In good hands, I do not see that it would do any harm. If it got into bad hands, it would be very bad.

Q. If it got into bad hands, it would wreck the country?

A. Yes; but I do not believe it could get into bad hands.

Q. You admit that if this concentration, to the point to which it has gone, were by any action to get into bad hands, it would wreck the country?

A. I can not imagine such a condition.

Q. I thought you said so?

A. I said it could be bad, but I do not think it would wreck the country. I do not think bad hands could manage it. They could not retain the deposits nor the securities.

Q. I am not speaking of incompetent hands. We are speaking of this concentration which has come about and the power that it brings with it getting into the hands of very ambitious men, perhaps not over-scrupulous. You see a peril in that, do you not?

A. Yes.

Q. So that the safety, if you think there is safety in the situation, really lies in the personnel of the men?

A. Very much.

Q. Do you think that is a comfortable situation for a great country to be in?

A. Not entirely.

BIBLIOGRAPHICAL NOTE

THOSE interested in specialized literature on the growth of capitalized industry and "high finance" in the United States will find a useful summary in *The Coming of Age of American Business: Three Centuries of Enterprise, 1600–1900* (1971) by E. P. Douglas. An authoritative and readable account reflecting the social impact of industrialization has been written by Thomas C. Cochran and William Miller: *The Age of Enterprise: A Social History of Industrial America* (1942). Another work of considerable interest is *A Financial History of the United States* (1970) by Margaret G. Myers. In *The Robber Barons* (1934), Matthew Josephson takes an analytical look at the men who pioneered in financing major industrial enterprises between the end of the Civil War and the beginning of the First World War. Stewart H. Holbrook covers roughly the same era as he describes the days of Carnegie, Schwab, Morgan and Vanderbilt in *The Age of Moguls* (1953).

The men whose names are synonomous with the rise of capitalism in the United States have not been neglected by biographers. The classic study of the senior Rockefeller is *John D. Rockefeller: The Heroic Age of Americans* by the Pulitzer Prize winning historian Allan Nevins (2 volumes, 1940) from which William

Greenleaf edited an abridged version (1959). Another book worth reading is John T. Flynn's *God's Gold: The Story of Rockefeller and His Times* (1932, reprinted 1971). The entire Rockefeller family is chronicled by William Manchester in *A Rockefeller Family Portrait: From John D. to Nelson* (1959). A Rockefeller partner has his biographer in Mark D. Hirsch, the author of *William C. Whitney: Modern Warick* (1948 reprinted 1969).

The Standard Oil Company, so closely associated with the Rockefeller dynasty, was the subject of a two-volume study published in 1955 and 1956: *Pioneering in Big Business, 1882–1911* by Ralph W. and Muriel E. Hidy and *Resurgent Years, 1911–1927* by George S. Gibb and E. H. Knowlton. An earlier work by Ida M. Tarbell, *History of the Standard Oil Company* (1904, reprinted 1969) gives an excellent picture of the Standard Oil Trust.

The House of Morgan (1930) by Lewis Corey and a work by the same title by Edwin P. Hoyt, Jr. (1966) are good surveys of that banking house. George Wheeler in *Pierpont Morgan and Friends: The Anatomy of a Myth* (1973) considers Morgan a mediocre financier whose ability in business was questioned even by his father. *Morgan Family History* (1966) by French Morgan, a member of the family, is an interesting genealogy. A study of Junius S. Morgan's predecessor as head of the banking house is *George Peabody: A Biography* (1971) by Franklin Parker. In *The Rothchilds* (1962) Frederic Morton has written a penetrating analysis of this other powerful family of international bankers.

Andrew Carnegie has a number of solid biographers. The standard work on his life and times is *Life of Andrew Carnegie* (2 volumes, 1932, reprinted 1969) by Burton J. Hendrick, Pulitzer Prize winner. Two other able accounts are Louis M. Hacker's, *World of Andrew Carnegie, 1865–1901* (1968) and Joseph F. Wall's *Andrew Carnegie* (1970). The latter reveals many facets of the complex character and career of a man active in industry, philanthropy, pacifism, politics and education. A useful book on another giant in the steel industry is *The Life of Elbert H. Gary: The Story of Steel* (1925) by Ida M. Tarbell.

Julius Grodinsky writes of the financier in *Jay Gould: His Business Career* (1957) while the entire family is treated by Edwin P. Hoyt, Jr. in *The Goulds* (1969). In 1936, Henrietta M. Larson gave us the life of the promoter and banker, in *Jay Cooke: Private Banker* (reprint 1969).

The famed railroad man and financier is dealt with in *E. H. Harriman* (2 volumes, 1922) by George Kennan. Two other railroad magnates are chronicled in Stewart H. Holbrook's *James J. Hill* (1955) and the book by James B. Hedges, *Henry Villard and the Railroads of the Northwest* (1930).

A good account of the activities of the War Industries Board is given in the autobiography of Bernard M. Baruch *My Own Story* (1957).

An interesting sidelight on the life styles of these men of capital may be found in *Merchants and Masterpieces: The Story of the Metropolitan Museum of Art* by Calvin Tomkins (1970).

INDEX